FALL Baking

SOUTHERN HARVEST FAVORITES

BROOKE BELL

hm | books

FALL
Baking

SOUTHERN HARVEST FAVORITES

hm | books

PRESIDENT/CCO Brian Hart Hoffman
VICE PRESIDENT/EDITORIAL Cindy Smith Cooper
DIRECTOR OF EDITORIAL OPERATIONS Brooke Michael Bell
GROUP CREATIVE DIRECTOR Deanna Rippy Gardner
ART DIRECTOR Lynn Akin Elkins

EDITORIAL

CREATIVE DIRECTOR/PHOTOGRAPHY Mac Jamieson
PROJECT EDITOR Anna Theoktisto
RECIPE EDITOR Fran Jensen
EDITORIAL ASSISTANT Alice Deters
COPY EDITOR Avery Hurt
SENIOR DIGITAL IMAGING SPECIALIST Delisa McDaniel
DIGITAL IMAGING SPECIALIST Clark Densmore
SENIOR PHOTOGRAPHERS John O'Hagan, Marcy Black Simpson
PHOTOGRAPHERS Jim Bathie, William Dickey, Stephanie Welbourne
ASSISTANT PHOTOGRAPHER Caroline Smith
FOOD STYLISTS AND RECIPE DEVELOPERS
  Mary-Claire Britton, Melissa Gray, Kathleen Kanen, Janet Lambert, Vanessa
  Rocchio, Emily Turner, Loren Wood
TEST KITCHEN ASSISTANT Anita Simpson Spain

hm
hoffmanmedia

CHAIRMAN OF THE BOARD/CEO Phyllis Hoffman DePiano
PRESIDENT/COO Eric W. Hoffman
PRESIDENT/CCO Brian Hart Hoffman
EXECUTIVE VICE PRESIDENT/CFO Mary P. Cummings
EXECUTIVE VICE PRESIDENT/OPERATIONS & MANUFACTURING
  Greg Baugh
VICE PRESIDENT/DIGITAL MEDIA Jon Adamson
VICE PRESIDENT/EDITORIAL Cindy Smith Cooper
VICE PRESIDENT/INTEGRATED MARKETING SOLUTIONS
  Ray Reed
VICE PRESIDENT/ADMINISTRATION Lynn Lee Terry

Hoffman Media
1900 International Park Drive, Suite 50
Birmingham, Alabama 35243
hoffmanmedia.com

ISBN: 978-1-940772-34-9
Printed in China

TO MY
MOTHER,
WHO TAUGHT
ME THAT
FALL REALLY
IS THE
BEST SEASON

Contents

Introduction

MORE THAN ANY OTHER SEASON,
THE FLAVORS OF FALL—CARAMEL, APPLE, SWEET
POTATO, CINNAMON, AND PUMPKIN SPICE—
INSPIRE OUR BAKING AND FILL OUR KITCHENS
WITH THE WARM AROMAS THAT USHER IN THIS
MOST-CELEBRATED TIME OF YEAR.

FALL BAKING

Golden Goodness

Caramel and maple syrup coat the season's desserts with comfort

CRANBERRY-CARAMEL PECAN CAKE

MAKES 1 (9-INCH) CAKE

1 cup unsalted butter, softened
2 cups firmly packed light brown sugar
3 tablespoons unsulphured molasses
3 large eggs
2 cups all-purpose flour
½ cup finely chopped pecans
1 teaspoon baking powder
1 teaspoon kosher salt
½ cup whole milk
2 teaspoons vanilla extract
Cranberry-Pecan Filling (recipe follows)
Molasses-Caramel Frosting (recipe follows)
Garnish: halved fresh cranberries

1. Preheat oven to 350°. Spray 2 (9-inch) round cake pans with baking spray with flour. Line bottom of pans with parchment paper, and spray pans again.

2. In a large bowl, beat butter, brown sugar, and molasses with a mixer at medium speed until fluffy, 3 to 4 minutes, stopping to scrape sides of bowl. Add eggs, one at a time, beating well after each addition.

3. In a medium bowl, whisk together flour, pecans, baking powder, and salt. Gradually add flour mixture to butter mixture alternately with milk, beginning and ending with flour mixture, beating just until combined after each addition. Beat in vanilla. Divide batter between prepared pans, smoothing tops with an offset spatula.

4. Bake until a wooden pick inserted in center comes out clean, 25 to 30 minutes. Let cool in pans for 10 minutes. Remove from pans, and let cool completely on wire racks.

5. Spread Cranberry-Pecan Filling between layers. Spread Molasses-Caramel Frosting on top and sides of cake. Garnish with cranberries, if desired. Cover and refrigerate for up to 3 days.

CRANBERRY-PECAN FILLING
MAKES ABOUT 1¼ CUPS

½ cup sugar
⅓ cup dark corn syrup
3 tablespoons unsalted butter, melted
1 large egg
½ teaspoon vanilla extract
⅔ cup fresh or frozen cranberries
½ cup chopped pecans

1. In a medium saucepan, stir together sugar, corn syrup, melted butter, egg, and vanilla until smooth. Stir in cranberries and pecans. Bring to a boil over medium-high heat, stirring frequently. Reduce heat to medium-low; simmer, stirring occasionally, until thickened, 6 to 8 minutes. Let cool to room temperature.

MOLASSES-CARAMEL FROSTING
MAKES ABOUT 5 CUPS

1 cup firmly packed light brown sugar
¼ cup water
2 tablespoons unsulphured molasses
½ teaspoon kosher salt
1½ cups unsalted butter, softened and divided
½ (8-ounce) package cream cheese, softened
3 cups confectioners' sugar

1. In a small saucepan, bring brown sugar, ¼ cup water, molasses, and salt to a boil over medium-high heat. Cook, stirring constantly, until sugar dissolves, about 2 minutes. Remove from heat; stir in ½ cup butter. Let cool completely.

2. In a large bowl, beat cooled brown sugar mixture, cream cheese, and remaining 1 cup butter with a mixer at medium speed until creamy. With mixer on low speed, gradually add confectioners' sugar, beating until combined. Refrigerate until thickened, about 1 hour.

APPLE GALETTES

MAKES 6

1¼ pounds Granny Smith apples
   (about 3 to 4 apples), peeled, cored,
   and sliced ¼ inch thick
1 tablespoon fresh lemon juice
1 tablespoon vanilla extract
¾ cup granulated sugar
2 tablespoons all-purpose flour
1 tablespoon cornstarch
½ teaspoon ground cinnamon
¼ teaspoon ground nutmeg
⅛ teaspoon salt
1 (14.1-ounce) package refrigerated
   piecrusts
Pecan Frangipane (recipe follows)
1 large egg, lightly beaten
1 tablespoon water
2 tablespoons coarse sugar
Garnish: whipped topping, Caramel Sauce
   (see page 132)

1. Preheat oven to 350°. Line a rimmed baking
sheet with parchment paper.
2. In a large bowl, combine apples, lemon juice,
and vanilla. In a small bowl, whisk together
granulated sugar, flour, cornstarch, cinnamon,
nutmeg, and salt. Add sugar mixture to apples,
tossing to coat each slice.
3. On a lightly floured surface, unroll half of
dough. Using a pastry brush, lightly coat with
water. Place remaining dough on top, pressing
to seal. Roll dough to ⅛-inch thickness. Cut
6 (6-inch) rounds from dough. Place rounds on
prepared pan. Spread each dough round with
1 to 1½ tablespoons Pecan Frangipane, leaving
a 2-inch border.

4. Strain apples, and arrange on top of filling,
leaving a 2-inch border. Wrap remaining dough
around apples in an overlapping fashion. In a small
bowl, whisk together egg and 1 tablespoon water.
Using a pastry brush, lightly coat each galette
with egg wash. Sprinkle each with coarse sugar.
5. Bake until golden brown, 25 to 30 minutes.
Remove from oven, and let cool slightly. Serve
warm with whipped topping and Caramel
Sauce, if desired. Cover and refrigerate for up to
3 days.

PECAN FRANGIPANE
MAKES 1½ CUPS

1 cup sugar
1 cup pecan halves
1 cup butter, softened
2 large eggs
1 teaspoon vanilla extract
¼ teaspoon salt

1. In the work bowl of a food processor, pulse
together sugar and pecans until finely ground.
Add butter, and pulse to combine. Add eggs,
one at a time, pulsing well after each addition.
Add vanilla and salt, and continue to pulse until
smooth. Cover and refrigerate for 1 hour.

Praline Custards with Pecan-Crackle Topping

MAKES 5 SERVINGS

2   cups heavy whipping cream
1   cup toasted pecans, chopped
½   vanilla bean, split lengthwise, seeds scraped
     and reserved
6   large egg yolks
⅓   cup sugar
⅛   teaspoon kosher salt
Pecan-Crackle Topping (recipe follows)

1. Preheat oven to 180°. Place 5 (4-ounce) ramekins on a rimmed baking sheet.
2. In a medium saucepan, bring cream, pecans, vanilla bean, and reserved vanilla bean seeds to a boil over medium heat. Remove from heat, and let stand for 30 minutes.
3. Strain mixture through a fine-mesh sieve into a medium bowl, discarding solids. Return mixture to saucepan.
4. In a medium bowl, whisk together egg yolks, sugar, and salt until combined. Add hot cream mixture to egg mixture in a slow, steady stream, whisking constantly, until fully combined. Strain mixture through a fine-mesh sieve, and divide among prepared ramekins.
5. Bake until centers are set, about 1 hour and 45 minutes. Let cool to room temperature. Refrigerate until chilled, about 4 hours. Sprinkle with Pecan-Crackle Topping.

Pecan-Crackle Topping
MAKES ABOUT 2 CUPS

1   cup pecan halves, toasted
1   cup sugar
¼   cup water

1. Line a rimmed baking sheet with parchment paper. Place pecans on prepared pan.
2. In a small saucepan, bring sugar and ¼ cup water to a boil over medium-high heat. Cook, stirring occasionally, until sugar turns amber in color, about 20 minutes.
3. Pour hot sugar mixture over pecans. Let cool completely, about 20 minutes. Transfer hardened mixture to a cutting board; chop into small pieces. Store in an airtight container for up to 1 week.

PECAN STICKY ROLLS

MAKES 12

Dough:
3½ cups all-purpose flour, divided
1 (0.25-ounce) package active dry yeast
½ cup whole milk
½ cup sour cream
⅓ cup butter, softened and cubed
⅓ cup sugar
½ teaspoon salt
1 teaspoon vanilla extract
1 large egg, lightly beaten

Filling:
¼ cup butter, softened
¼ cup sugar
2 teaspoons ground cinnamon
1 teaspoon orange zest
1 teaspoon all-purpose flour
⅛ teaspoon salt

Glaze:
½ cup firmly packed light brown sugar
⅓ cup butter
⅓ cup light corn syrup
⅛ teaspoon salt
½ cup toasted pecans, chopped

1. For dough: In a large bowl, combine 1½ cups flour and yeast. In a medium saucepan, combine milk, sour cream, butter, sugar, and salt. Cook over medium heat, stirring occasionally, until a candy thermometer registers 120°. Pour over flour mixture. Add vanilla and egg, stirring well. Gradually stir in flour (about 1½ cups) until a soft dough forms and pulls away from sides of bowl.

2. Turn out dough onto a lightly floured surface, and knead until smooth and elastic, 5 to 7 minutes, adding remaining ½ cup flour, 2 teaspoons at a time, as needed. Spray a large bowl with cooking spray. Place dough in bowl, turning to grease top. Cover and let rise in a warm, draft-free place (75°) until doubled in size, about 1 hour and 15 minutes.

3. Lightly punch down dough. Cover and let stand for 5 minutes. On a lightly floured surface, roll dough into a 14x10-inch rectangle.

4. For filling: Spread butter onto dough. In a small bowl, stir together sugar, cinnamon, zest, flour, and salt. Sprinkle over butter; gently press mixture into dough. Starting at one long side, roll up dough, jelly-roll style, and press edge to seal. Place seam side down, and cut into 12 rolls. Place rolls in a 10-inch cast-iron skillet. Cover and let rise in a warm, draft-free place (75°) until doubled in size, about 45 minutes.

5. Preheat oven to 350°. Uncover rolls. Bake until golden brown, about 25 minutes. Let cool in pan for 30 minutes.

6. For glaze: In a medium saucepan, combine brown sugar, butter, corn syrup, and salt. Bring to a boil over medium heat, stirring frequently. Cook for 1 minute, stirring frequently. Stir in pecans; let stand for 3 minutes. Pour over rolls.

Quick-and-Easy Caramel Cake

MAKES 10 TO 12 SERVINGS

½ cup unsalted butter, softened
½ cup granulated sugar
½ cup firmly packed light brown sugar
3 large eggs
2 teaspoons vanilla extract
2 cups cake flour
2 teaspoons baking powder
½ teaspoon salt
¾ cup half-and-half
1 (12-ounce) jar plus ¼ cup caramel topping, divided
Easy Cream Cheese Frosting (recipe follows)

1. Preheat oven to 350°. Lightly spray a 13x9-inch baking pan with baking spray with flour.
2. In a large bowl, beat butter and sugars with a mixer at high speed until fluffy, 3 to 4 minutes, stopping to scrape sides of bowl. Add eggs, one at a time, beating well after each addition. Beat in vanilla.
3. In a medium bowl, whisk together flour, baking powder, and salt. Gradually add flour mixture to butter mixture alternately with half-and-half, beginning and ending with flour mixture, beating just until combined after each addition. Spread batter in prepared pan, smoothing top with an offset spatula.
4. Bake until a wooden pick inserted in center comes out clean, 25 to 30 minutes. Using the handle of a wooden spoon, poke holes in top of warm cake. Pour ¼ cup caramel topping over cake. Let cake stand at room temperature to absorb caramel and cool completely, about 2 hours.

5. Spread Easy Cream Cheese Frosting over cooled cake. Pour remaining 1 jar caramel topping over frosting. Pull a butter knife through caramel topping to swirl.

Easy Cream Cheese Frosting
MAKES ABOUT 4 CUPS

2 (8-ounce) packages cream cheese, softened
1 teaspoon vanilla extract
5 cups confectioners' sugar

1. In a large bowl, beat cream cheese and vanilla with a mixer at medium-high speed until creamy, about 2 minutes. Gradually add confectioners' sugar, beating until smooth.

Be sure to let the cake cool
completely before adding
Easy Cream Cheese Frosting
to prevent the frosting
from melting.

CARAMEL LAYER CAKE

MAKES 1 (9-INCH) CAKE

1 cup butter, softened
2 cups sugar
4 large eggs
3 cups self-rising flour
1 cup whole buttermilk
1½ teaspoons vanilla extract
Caramel Frosting (recipe follows)
⅓ cup reserved caramel from Caramel Frosting
Garnish: toasted pecan halves

1. Preheat oven to 350°. Spray 3 (9-inch) round cake pans with baking spray with flour. Line bottom of pans with parchment paper, and spray pans again.
2. In a large bowl, beat butter and sugar with a mixer at medium speed until fluffy, 3 to 4 minutes, stopping to scrape sides of bowl. Add eggs, one at a time, beating well after each addition. Gradually add flour to butter mixture alternately with buttermilk, beginning and ending with flour, beating just until combined after each addition. Beat in vanilla. Divide batter among prepared pans, smoothing tops with an offset spatula.
3. Bake until a wooden pick inserted in center comes out clean, 25 to 30 minutes. Let cool in pans for 10 minutes. Remove from pans, and let cool completely on wire racks.
4. Spread Caramel Frosting between layers and on top and sides of cake. Drizzle with ⅓ cup reserved caramel from Caramel Frosting. Garnish with pecans, if desired.

CARAMEL FROSTING
MAKES ABOUT 5 CUPS

2 cups sugar
¼ cup water
2 tablespoons light corn syrup
½ cup cold butter, cubed
1 cup hot heavy whipping cream
1 cup butter, softened
6 cups confectioners' sugar, sifted

1. In a large heavy-bottomed saucepan, place sugar. In a small bowl, whisk together ¼ cup water and corn syrup. Pour over sugar, stirring just until sugar is moistened. Cook over medium-high heat, without stirring, until mixture is golden brown. (While caramel cooks, brush any sugar crystals on sides of pan with a pastry brush dipped in water.) Remove from heat.
2. Using a long-handled wooden spoon, add cold butter. Stir until butter melts. (Mixture will foam.) Slowly add hot cream, stirring until smooth. (If mixture does not get smooth, cook over low heat, stirring until smooth.) Let mixture cool until slightly warm, about 1 hour, stirring occasionally. Reserve ⅓ cup caramel to drizzle over assembled cake.
3. Pour caramel mixture into a large bowl. Add softened butter, and beat with a mixer at medium speed until smooth. With mixer on low speed, gradually add confectioners' sugar, beating until smooth. Place a piece of plastic wrap on surface of frosting. Let stand until frosting has reached a spreadable consistency, about 10 minutes.

Maple, Bacon, and Bourbon Cupcakes

MAKES 24

1 cup butter, softened
1¼ cups sugar
3 large eggs
⅓ cup whole milk
⅓ cup bourbon
2 teaspoons vanilla extract
2⅓ cups self-rising flour
Maple Glaze (recipe follows)
3 slices bacon, cooked and crumbled

1. Preheat oven to 350°. Line 24 muffin cups with paper liners.
2. In a large bowl, beat butter and sugar with a mixer at medium speed until fluffy, 3 to 4 minutes, stopping to scrape sides of bowl. Add eggs, one at a time, beating well after each addition.
3. In a small bowl, combine milk, bourbon, and vanilla. Gradually add flour to butter mixture alternately with milk mixture, beginning and ending with flour, beating just until combined after each addition. Divide batter among prepared muffin cups.
4. Bake until a wooden pick inserted in center comes out clean, 18 to 20 minutes. Let cool in pan for 5 minutes. Remove from pan, and let cool completely on a wire rack.
5. Spread Maple Glaze over cupcakes; top with bacon.

Maple Glaze
MAKES ABOUT ½ CUP

1½ cups confectioners' sugar, sifted
4 to 5 tablespoons maple syrup
¾ teaspoon fresh lemon juice

1. In a medium bowl, combine confectioners' sugar, 4 tablespoons maple syrup, and lemon juice; whisk until smooth. Add remaining 1 tablespoon maple syrup if mixture is too thick.

CARAMEL OATMEAL CREAM PIES

MAKES ABOUT 14 SANDWICH COOKIES

Cookies:

¾ cup unsalted butter, softened
1½ cups firmly packed dark brown sugar
1 large egg
3 cups quick-cooking oats (not instant)
1 cup all-purpose flour
2 tablespoons light corn syrup
½ teaspoon salt
½ teaspoon baking soda

Cream Filling:

¼ cup unsalted butter
2 tablespoons cream cheese, softened
1 cup confectioners' sugar
1 cup marshmallow crème

Caramel Sauce, chilled (recipe on page 132)

1. Preheat oven to 350°. Line a baking sheet with parchment paper.
2. For cookies: In a large bowl, beat butter and brown sugar with a mixer at medium speed until fluffy, 3 to 4 minutes, stopping to scrape sides of bowl. Add egg, beating until combined. Add oats, flour, corn syrup, salt, and baking soda, beating until combined. Using a 1-inch spring-loaded ice cream scoop or tablespoon, drop dough 1 inch apart on prepared pan.

3. Bake until just set, about 10 minutes. Let cool on pan for 2 minutes. Remove from pan, and let cool completely on a wire rack.
4. For cream filling: In a small bowl, beat butter and cream cheese with a mixer at medium speed until combined. Add confectioners' sugar and marshmallow crème, beating until smooth. Cover and refrigerate until chilled, about 1 hour.
5. Spread cream filling onto flat side of half of cookies. Spread about 2 teaspoons Caramel Sauce onto flat side of remaining cookies. Top cream-coated cookies with caramel-coated cookies. Cover and refrigerate for up to 2 days.

CHOCOLATE-CARAMEL TART

MAKES 4 TO 6 SERVINGS

½ (14.1-ounce) package refrigerated piecrusts

Chocolate Filling:
1 (4-ounce) bar semisweet chocolate, finely chopped
⅓ cup heavy whipping cream
1 tablespoon unsalted butter
1 tablespoon light corn syrup

Caramel Filling:
¾ cup sugar
2 tablespoons water
2 tablespoons light corn syrup
3 tablespoons cold unsalted butter
¼ teaspoon salt
½ cup heavy whipping cream
2 tablespoons bourbon (optional)
½ teaspoon flaked or kosher salt

1. Preheat oven to 450°.
2. On a lightly floured surface, roll dough into a 15x6-inch rectangle. Press dough into a 13x4-inch removeable-bottom tart pan. Fold edges of dough under. Prick dough with a fork 5 to 7 times.
3. Bake until lightly browned, about 8 minutes. Let cool completely on a wire rack.
4. For chocolate filling: In a medium bowl, place chocolate. In a small microwave-safe bowl, place cream and butter. Microwave until hot but not boiling, about 30 seconds. Add cream mixture and corn syrup to chocolate, stirring until chocolate melts and mixture is smooth. Pour into prepared crust, smoothing top with an offset spatula. Refrigerate until set, about 45 minutes.
5. For caramel filling: In a medium heavy saucepan, sprinkle sugar in an even layer. In a small bowl, stir together 2 tablespoons water and corn syrup until combined. Pour over sugar, stirring just until moistened. Cook over medium-high heat, without stirring, until golden brown. Remove from heat. Add butter and salt, whisking until butter melts.
6. In a small microwave-safe bowl, place cream and bourbon (if using). Microwave until hot but not boiling, about 30 seconds. Whisk into caramel. (Mixture will foam.) Cook over low heat for 4 minutes, stirring frequently. Remove from heat; pour into a bowl. Place bowl in a larger bowl of ice. Let stand until completely cooled, about 20 minutes, stirring occasionally. Spread onto chocolate filling. Refrigerate until set, about 30 minutes. Sprinkle with salt just before serving.

CRANBERRY-CARAMEL TART

MAKES 1 (9-INCH) TART

Crust:
1   cup all-purpose flour
⅔   cup confectioners' sugar
½   cup toasted pecans
½   teaspoon kosher salt
½   cup unsalted butter, softened and cubed

Filling:
1   cup sugar
½   cup water
½   cup unsalted butter, softened
⅔   cup heavy whipping cream, warmed
1   teaspoon vanilla extract
2   cups pecan halves
2   cups frozen cranberries
¼   teaspoon kosher salt

1. Preheat oven to 350°.
2. For crust: In the work bowl of a food processor, pulse together flour, confectioners' sugar, pecans, and salt until finely ground. With processor running, gradually add butter. Process until dough comes together. Press dough into bottom and up sides of a 9-inch removable-bottom tart pan. Freeze for 10 minutes. Prick bottom of crust 10 times with a fork. Place a piece of parchment paper over crust, letting ends extend over edges of pan. Add pie weights.
3. Bake for 20 minutes. Carefully remove paper and weights. Bake until lightly browned, about 5 minutes more. Let cool on a wire rack.
4. For filling: In a medium saucepan, combine sugar and ½ cup water. Cook over medium heat, whisking often, until a candy thermometer registers 340° and mixture is amber in color, about 10 minutes. Remove from heat. Carefully whisk in butter until melted. (Mixture will boil vigorously.) Add cream and vanilla, whisking until smooth. Stir in pecans, cranberries, and salt. Spoon mixture into prepared crust.
5. Bake until bubbly, 20 to 25 minutes. Let cool to room temperature. Refrigerate for at least 30 minutes before slicing.

Harvest Fruit

APPLES AND PEARS REIGN AS
AUTUMN'S MOST-BELOVED PRIZE

Candied Apple-Pear Bundt Cake

MAKES 10 TO 12 SERVINGS

3   cups sugar, divided
½   cup cane syrup
1½   cups plus 2 tablespoons unsalted butter,
       softened and divided
2   large Granny Smith apples, peeled, cored,
       and sliced
2   Bosc pears, peeled, cored, and sliced
5   large eggs
3   cups all-purpose flour
2   teaspoons ground cinnamon
1   teaspoon grated fresh nutmeg
1   teaspoon kosher salt
½   teaspoon baking soda
1   cup sour cream
2   teaspoons vanilla extract
Cane Syrup Glaze (recipe follows)

1. Preheat oven to 325°. Spray a 15-cup Bundt pan with baking spray with flour.
2. In a large skillet, bring 1 cup sugar and cane syrup to a boil over medium-high heat, stirring constantly, until sugar dissolves, about 2 minutes. Stir in 2 tablespoons butter until melted. Add apples and pears, stirring to combine. Reduce heat to medium; cook, stirring occasionally, until fruit softens, about 12 minutes. Remove from heat, and let cool completely.
3. In a large bowl, beat remaining 1½ cups butter and remaining 2 cups sugar with a mixer at medium speed until fluffy, 3 to 4 minutes, stopping to scrape sides of bowl. Add eggs, one at a time, beating well after each addition.
4. In a medium bowl, stir together flour, cinnamon, nutmeg, salt, and baking soda. Gradually add flour mixture to butter mixture alternately with sour cream, beginning and ending with flour mixture, beating just until combined after each addition. Beat in vanilla.
5. Reserve ⅔ cup syrup from fruit mixture for Cane Syrup Glaze; set aside. Gently fold remaining syrup and fruit mixture into batter. Spoon batter into prepared pan.
6. Bake until a wooden pick inserted near center comes out clean, about 1 hour and 10 minutes. Let cool in pan for 10 minutes. Remove from pan, and let cool completely on a wire rack. Drizzle with Cane Syrup Glaze.

Cane Syrup Glaze

In a small bowl, stir together ⅔ cup reserved syrup from fruit mixture, 2 cups confectioners' sugar, and 2 tablespoons whole buttermilk until smooth.

Pear-Almond Cake

MAKES 6 SERVINGS

1 cup butter, softened
1½ cups granulated sugar
3 large eggs
2 cups all-purpose flour
¼ teaspoon salt
⅓ cup whole milk
½ teaspoon almond extract
½ teaspoon vanilla extract
1 large red pear, cut into 12 thin slices
½ cup sliced almonds
Confectioners' sugar

1. Preheat oven to 350°. Spray a 9-inch cast-iron skillet with baking spray with flour.

2. In a large bowl, beat butter and granulated sugar with a mixer at medium speed until fluffy, 3 to 4 minutes, stopping to scrape sides of bowl. Add eggs, one at a time, beating well after each addition.

3. In a small bowl, whisk together flour and salt. Gradually add flour mixture to butter mixture alternately with milk, beginning and ending with flour mixture, beating just until combined after each addition. Beat in almond extract and vanilla. Spoon batter into prepared pan. Place pears cut side down in a pinwheel fashion over batter.

4. Bake until lightly browned, about 20 minutes. Sprinkle with almonds, and bake until a wooden pick inserted in center comes out clean, about 10 minutes more. Let cool in pan for 15 minutes. Sprinkle with confectioners' sugar, and serve warm.

RED WINE-POACHED PEAR TART

MAKES 1 (14X4-INCH) TART

Almond Crust (recipe follows)
3   cups dry red wine, such as Zinfandel
½   cup granulated sugar
2   star anise
5   small Bartlett or Anjou pears,
    peeled, halved, and cored
Almond Cream, chilled (recipe follows)
Garnish: toasted sliced almonds,
    confectioners' sugar

1. Preheat oven to 350°.
2. Remove Almond Crust from freezer. Peel off 1 sheet of parchment paper. Place dough, parchment side up, on a 14x4-inch removable-bottom tart pan; carefully peel off remaining parchment. Gently press dough into bottom and up sides of pan. (If dough cracks, press it back together.) Place a piece of parchment in bottom of tart shell, letting ends extend over edges. Fill with pie weights. Bake for 15 minutes. Remove parchment and weights. Let cool on a wire rack. Reduce oven temperature to 325°.
3. In a medium saucepan, bring wine, granulated sugar, and star anise to a boil over high heat. Boil for 5 minutes; reduce heat to low. Add pears to saucepan; cover and simmer until pears are tender, about 20 minutes. Carefully remove pears from pan, and let cool completely.
4. Spread Almond Cream in bottom of cooled tart shell. Arrange cooled poached pears over Almond Cream.
5. Bake until center is set, 40 to 45 minutes. Let cool completely before cutting. Garnish with almonds and confectioners' sugar, if desired.

ALMOND CRUST
MAKES 1 (16X6-INCH) CRUST

1   cup cake flour
½   teaspoon baking powder
½   cup unsalted butter, softened
½   cup sugar
1   large egg
½   cup sliced almonds, finely chopped
¼   teaspoon kosher salt

1. In a medium bowl, sift together flour and baking powder; set aside.
2. In a large bowl, beat butter and sugar with a mixer at medium speed until creamy, about 2 minutes. Add egg, beating well. Add flour mixture, almonds, and salt, beating until well combined.
3. On a work surface, place a large sheet of parchment paper. Place dough in middle of parchment; top with a second sheet of parchment. Roll dough between parchment into a 16x6-inch rectangle. Freeze until firm, about 15 minutes.

ALMOND CREAM
MAKES ABOUT 1 CUP

½   cup almond flour
¼   cup plus 1 tablespoon sugar
¼   cup unsalted butter, softened
1   large egg yolk
2   teaspoons all-purpose flour
¼   teaspoon lemon zest
¼   teaspoon kosher salt
¼   teaspoon almond extract

1. In a medium bowl, beat all ingredients with a mixer at medium speed until pale in color and fluffy, about 3 minutes. Cover and refrigerate for at least 3 hours.

CRANBERRY-APPLE UPSIDE-DOWN JOHNNYCAKE

MAKES ABOUT 8 SERVINGS

⅓ cup unsalted butter
1 cup firmly packed light brown sugar
⅓ cup plus 3 tablespoons apple cider, divided
1½ large Granny Smith apples, peeled, cored, and sliced ¼ inch thick
1 teaspoon fresh lemon juice
½ cup sweetened dried cranberries
2 (8.5-ounce) packages corn muffin mix
2 large eggs
⅓ cup whole milk

1. Preheat oven to 350°. Spray a 9-inch round cake pan with baking spray with flour.
2. In a small saucepan, bring butter and brown sugar to a boil over medium heat, stirring until mixture pulls away from sides of pan, about 3 minutes. Stir in 3 tablespoons apple cider; cook 1 minute more. Pour into prepared pan. Let cool completely.
3. In a small bowl, stir together apples and lemon juice. Arrange apples in a circle over cooled caramel in pan, overlapping slightly. Top with cranberries.
4. In a medium bowl, stir together corn muffin mix, eggs, milk, and remaining ⅓ cup apple cider until well combined. Pour batter over fruit, gently smoothing top with an offset spatula.
5. Bake until a wooden pick inserted in center comes out clean, 30 to 35 minutes. Let cool in pan for 30 minutes. Run a knife around edges of pan to loosen, and invert onto a serving platter.

THIS VERSATILE DOUGH FREEZES
BEAUTIFULLY. PLACE WRAPPED
DOUGH IN A HEAVY-DUTY
RESEALABLE PLASTIC BAG, AND
FREEZE FOR UP TO 3 MONTHS.

Apple Hand Pies with Caramel Sauce

MAKES 10

Puff Pastry-Style Pie Dough (recipe follows)
1   cup peeled and diced Granny Smith apple
1   teaspoon all-purpose flour
⅛   teaspoon lemon zest
¾   teaspoon fresh lemon juice
¼   teaspoon ground cinnamon
½   cup firmly packed light brown sugar
2   tablespoons unsalted butter, melted
½   teaspoon vanilla extract
⅛   teaspoon kosher salt
1   large egg, lightly beaten
1   tablespoon water
Coarse sugar
Caramel Sauce (recipe on page 132)

1. Preheat oven to 425°. Line 2 baking sheets with parchment paper.
2. On a lightly floured surface, unfold Puff Pastry-Style Pie Dough; roll into a 15x15-inch square. Using a 3-inch round cutter, cut 20 rounds, rerolling scraps as necessary. Place 5 rounds on each prepared pan; reserve remaining 10 rounds.
3. In a medium bowl, stir together apple, flour, lemon zest, lemon juice, and cinnamon. In a small bowl, stir together brown sugar, melted butter, vanilla, and salt. In another small bowl, stir together egg and 1 tablespoon water.
4. Place 1 heaping tablespoonful of apple mixture onto center of 1 round; top with 1 teaspoon brown sugar mixture. Brush egg wash around edges of round. Top with 1 round, pressing and crimping with a fork to seal edges. Brush top with egg

wash, and sprinkle with coarse sugar. Cut 3 small vents in top. Repeat with remaining rounds, filling, and egg wash.
5. Bake until golden brown, 15 to 18 minutes. Let cool on a wire rack. Drizzle with Caramel Sauce.

PUFF PASTRY-STYLE PIE DOUGH
MAKES DOUGH FOR 10 HAND PIES

2   cups all-purpose flour
½   teaspoon kosher salt
½   teaspoon baking powder
1   cup cold unsalted butter, cubed
½   cup whole buttermilk, chilled

1. In a large bowl, whisk together flour, salt, and baking powder. Using a pastry blender, cut in butter until mixture is crumbly. Add buttermilk, stirring until combined.
2. Turn out dough onto a lightly floured surface, kneading briefly until dough comes together. Shape dough into a log.
3. Roll dough into a 10x8-inch rectangle. Lightly flour both sides, and fold dough into thirds, letter-style. Rotate dough 90 degrees, and roll into another 10x8-inch rectangle. Lightly flour both sides of dough. Fold into thirds; wrap tightly in plastic wrap. Refrigerate for at least 30 minutes.

APPLE-WALNUT CAKE

MAKES 12 TO 14 SERVINGS

Cake:
- 1 cup plus 2 tablespoons butter, softened and divided
- 1 cup chopped Granny Smith apple
- 1 cup chopped Fuji apple
- 1 cup granulated sugar
- 1 cup firmly packed dark brown sugar
- 6 large eggs
- 1 teaspoon vanilla extract
- 2½ cups all-purpose flour
- 1 teaspoon baking powder
- 1 teaspoon baking soda
- ¼ teaspoon salt
- 1 cup sour cream
- ½ cup toasted walnuts, chopped

Glaze:
- ¼ cup unsalted butter
- ½ cup firmly packed light brown sugar
- ¼ cup heavy whipping cream
- ½ teaspoon vanilla extract

1. Preheat oven to 350°. Spray a 10- to 15-cup Bundt pan with baking spray with flour.
2. For cake: In a large nonstick skillet, melt 2 tablespoons butter over medium heat. Add apples. Cook, stirring frequently, until tender, 4 to 5 minutes. Set aside.
3. In a large bowl, beat sugars and remaining 1 cup butter with a mixer at medium speed until fluffy, 3 to 4 minutes, stopping to scrape sides of bowl. Add eggs, one at a time, beating well after each addition. Beat in vanilla.

4. In a medium bowl, sift together flour, baking powder, baking soda, and salt. Gradually add flour mixture to butter mixture alternately with sour cream, beginning and ending with flour mixture, beating just until combined after each addition. Fold in apples and walnuts. Spoon into prepared pan.
5. Bake until a wooden pick inserted near center comes out clean, 40 to 50 minutes. Let cool in pan for 10 minutes. Remove from pan, and let cool completely on a wire rack.
6. For glaze: In a medium saucepan, melt butter over medium heat. Add brown sugar and cream. Cook, stirring constantly, until smooth, 2 to 3 minutes. Add vanilla, stirring to combine. Drizzle glaze over top and sides of cooled cake.

Skillet Apple-Streusel Pie

MAKES 1 (10-INCH) PIE

Dough:
1⅓ cups all-purpose flour
2   teaspoons sugar
½   teaspoon salt
½   cup cold unsalted butter, cubed
3 to 4 tablespoons cold apple cider

Streusel:
½   cup old-fashioned oats
⅓   cup all-purpose flour
2   tablespoons firmly packed light
     brown sugar
⅛   teaspoon salt
2   tablespoons unsalted butter, melted

Filling:
6   cups sliced Gala apple (about 2½ pounds)
⅓   cup granulated sugar
⅓   cup firmly packed light brown sugar
2   tablespoons cornstarch
1½   teaspoons apple pie spice
⅛   teaspoon salt
1   tablespoon fresh lemon juice
Caramel Sauce (recipe on page 132)

1. For dough: In the work bowl of a food processor, pulse together flour, sugar, and salt. Add butter, pulsing until mixture is crumbly. With processor running, gradually add 3 tablespoons apple cider until a dough forms. Add remaining 1 tablespoon apple cider, if needed.

2. Turn out dough onto a lightly floured surface, and shape into a disk. Cover with plastic wrap, and refrigerate for 30 minutes. Remove from refrigerator 15 minutes before rolling.

3. Preheat oven to 375°.

4. For streusel: In a medium bowl, stir together oats, flour, brown sugar, and salt. Add melted butter, stirring until mixture is crumbly. Cover and refrigerate until ready to use or up to 5 days.

5. On a lightly floured surface, roll dough into a 13-inch circle. Transfer to a 10-inch cast-iron skillet, pressing into bottom and up sides. Fold edges under.

6. For filling: In a large bowl, stir together apples, sugars, cornstarch, apple pie spice, and salt. Sprinkle with lemon juice; stir to combine. Spoon apple mixture into prepared crust. Sprinkle with streusel.

7. Bake until crust is golden brown and apples are tender, about 45 minutes, loosely covering with foil during last 10 minutes of baking to prevent excess browning, if necessary. Drizzle with Caramel Sauce.

Upside-Down Apple Crisp Cake

MAKES 1 (10-INCH) CAKE

Cake:
½ cup plus ⅓ cup unsalted butter, softened and divided
1¾ cups firmly packed light brown sugar, divided
¾ teaspoon ground cinnamon, divided
¾ teaspoon ground nutmeg, divided
2 large Pink Lady or Honeycrisp apples, peeled, cored, and thinly sliced
1 large egg
1⅓ cups all-purpose flour
2 teaspoons baking powder
½ teaspoon kosher salt
⅓ cup whole milk
1 teaspoon vanilla extract

Crumble:
¼ cup firmly packed light brown sugar
¼ cup old-fashioned oats
3 tablespoons unsalted butter, softened
2 tablespoons all-purpose flour
⅛ teaspoon kosher salt

1. Preheat oven to 350°.
2. For cake: In a 10-inch cast-iron skillet, melt ⅓ cup butter over medium heat. Add ¾ cup brown sugar, ¼ teaspoon cinnamon, and ¼ teaspoon nutmeg, stirring to combine. Cook, stirring occasionally, until thickened, about 8 minutes. Remove from heat. Place apple slices over caramel in skillet.

3. In a large bowl, beat remaining ½ cup butter and remaining 1 cup brown sugar with a mixer at medium speed until fluffy, 3 to 4 minutes, stopping to scrape sides of bowl. Add egg, beating to combine.
4. In a medium bowl, stir together flour, baking powder, salt, remaining ½ teaspoon cinnamon, and remaining ½ teaspoon nutmeg. Gradually add flour mixture to butter mixture alternately with milk, beginning and ending with flour mixture, beating just until combined after each addition. Beat in vanilla. Spoon batter over apples in skillet, smoothing top with an offset spatula.
5. For crumble: In a small bowl, stir together brown sugar, oats, butter, flour, and salt until crumbly. Sprinkle over batter.
6. Bake until a wooden pick inserted in center comes out clean, about 40 minutes. Let cool in pan for 10 minutes. Carefully invert onto a flat serving plate.

CREAM CHEESE SWIRL BUNDT CAKE
MAKES ABOUT 12 SERVINGS

Cake:
1 (8-ounce) package cream cheese, softened
½ cup unsalted butter, softened
2 cups firmly packed light brown sugar
4 large eggs
3 cups self-rising flour
1 tablespoon apple pie spice
1 teaspoon vanilla extract

Swirl:
1 (8-ounce) package cream cheese, softened
¼ cup sugar
1 tablespoon whole milk
1 large egg

Apple Cider Syrup (recipe on page 133)

1. Preheat oven to 350°. Spray a 15-cup Bundt pan with baking spray with flour.
2. For cake: In a large bowl, beat cream cheese and butter with a mixer at medium speed until creamy. Add brown sugar, and beat until fluffy, 3 to 4 minutes, stopping to scrape sides of bowl. Add eggs, one at a time, beating well after each addition.
3. In a medium bowl, whisk together flour and apple pie spice. Gradually add flour mixture to butter mixture, beating at low speed just until combined. Beat in vanilla.
4. For swirl: In a medium bowl, beat cream cheese, sugar, and milk with a mixer at medium speed until smooth. Add egg; beat just until combined. Spoon half of batter into prepared pan. Spoon half of swirl mixture over batter, avoiding edges of pan. Repeat procedure; swirl with a knife. Tap pan on counter twice to release air bubbles.
5. Bake until a wooden pick inserted near center comes out clean, 42 to 44 minutes. Let cool in pan for 10 minutes. Remove from pan, and let cool completely on a wire rack. Place cake on a serving plate. Brush with Apple Cider Syrup; drizzle with desired amount of remaining syrup.

APPLE CIDER SYRUP
HAS A TART FLAVOR.
STIR IN 2 TABLESPOONS HONEY
OR MAPLE SYRUP AFTER BOILING,
IF DESIRED.

CIDER-GLAZED BAKED DOUGHNUTS

MAKES ABOUT 16

1 (0.25-ounce) package active dry yeast
¼ cup warm water (105° to 110°)
5 cups all-purpose flour, divided
1¼ cups warm whole milk (105° to 110°)
⅔ cup firmly packed light brown sugar
½ cup unsalted butter, softened
1 large egg
1 teaspoon kosher salt
1 teaspoon vanilla extract
½ cup unsalted butter, melted
¾ cup Apple Cider Syrup (recipe on page 133)
3 tablespoons granulated sugar

1. In a small bowl, stir together yeast and ¼ cup warm water. Let stand until mixture is foamy, about 5 minutes.
2. In the bowl of a stand mixer fitted with the paddle attachment, beat yeast mixture, 3½ cups flour, warm milk, brown sugar, softened butter, egg, salt, and vanilla at low speed until combined. (Some pieces of butter will remain.) Switch to dough hook attachment; gradually add remaining 1½ cups flour, beating until a dough forms and pulls away from sides of bowl. (Dough will be sticky.)
3. Turn out dough onto a lightly floured surface, and knead until dough forms a smooth ball, about 8 times. Spray a large bowl with cooking spray. Place dough in bowl, turning to grease top. Cover and let rise in a warm, draft-free place (75°) until doubled in size, about 1 hour and 15 minutes.
4. Line 2 large baking sheets with parchment paper.
5. Punch dough down. On a lightly floured surface, roll dough to ½-inch thickness. Using a doughnut cutter, cut doughnuts. Place 2 inches apart on prepared pans. Loosely cover, and let rise until puffy, 30 to 40 minutes.
6. Preheat oven to 375°. Uncover dough. Bake until lightly browned, about 12 minutes. Brush with melted butter. Drizzle with Apple Cider Syrup, and sprinkle with granulated sugar. Serve warm.

Pear-Almond Crostata

MAKES ABOUT 6 SERVINGS

Crust:
1⅓ cups all-purpose flour
2 tablespoons sugar
½ teaspoon salt
½ cup cold unsalted butter, cubed
5 to 6 tablespoons ice water

Filling:
2 tablespoons almond paste, crumbled
5 small Bartlett pears (about 2 pounds),
 peeled, cored, and sliced
2 tablespoons granulated sugar
2 teaspoons all-purpose flour
½ teaspoon ground ginger
⅛ teaspoon salt
1 tablespoon fresh lemon juice
1 large egg
1 teaspoon water
2 teaspoons turbinado sugar
Garnish: honey, toasted sliced almonds

1. For crust: In the work bowl of a food processor, pulse together flour, sugar, and salt. Add butter, pulsing until mixture is crumbly. Spoon flour mixture into a large bowl. Sprinkle ice water over flour mixture, 1 tablespoon at a time, tossing with a fork until dry ingredients are moistened.
2. Turn out dough onto a lightly floured surface, and knead just until dough is combined, 2 to 3 times. Shape dough into a disk, and wrap in plastic wrap. Refrigerate for 30 minutes.
3. Preheat oven to 375°. Line a baking sheet with parchment paper.
4. On a lightly floured surface, roll dough into a 12-inch circle. Transfer dough to prepared pan.
5. For filling: Sprinkle almond paste over dough, leaving a 2-inch border. In a large bowl, combine pears, granulated sugar, flour, ginger, and salt. Sprinkle lemon juice over pear mixture, tossing to combine. Arrange pear mixture over almond paste. Gently fold edges of dough over filling.
6. In a small bowl, whisk together egg and 1 teaspoon water. Brush egg wash over edges of dough; sprinkle with turbinado sugar.
7. Bake until crust is golden brown and filling is bubbly, about 40 minutes. Let cool on pan for 20 minutes. Garnish with honey and almonds, if desired.

Pumpkin & Sweet Potato

FROM PIES TO BISCUITS—FALL BAKING'S

RICHEST JEWELS SHINE

Pumpkin-Sweet Potato Bread

MAKES 1 (9X5-INCH) LOAF

1   cup all-purpose flour
¾   cup whole wheat flour
2   teaspoons pumpkin pie spice
1   teaspoon baking powder
1   teaspoon baking soda
½   teaspoon kosher salt
1   cup canned pumpkin
1   cup loosely packed grated sweet potato
1   (8-ounce) can crushed pineapple, drained
1   apple, grated and squeezed dry
¾   cup firmly packed light brown sugar
1   tablespoon grated fresh ginger
2   large eggs, lightly beaten
½   cup chopped sweetened dates
¼   cup coconut oil, melted
Maple-Bourbon Glaze (recipe follows)
Garnish: chopped pecans, orange zest

1. Preheat oven to 350°. Spray a 9x5-inch loaf pan with cooking spray.
2. In a large bowl, whisk together flours, pumpkin pie spice, baking powder, baking soda, and salt. Set aside.
3. In a medium bowl, stir together pumpkin, sweet potato, pineapple, apple, brown sugar, ginger, and eggs until combined. Make a well in center of dry ingredients. Add pumpkin mixture, stirring just until combined. Add dates and melted coconut oil, stirring to combine. Spoon into prepared pan, smoothing top with an offset spatula.
4. Bake until a wooden pick inserted in center comes out clean, 55 minutes to 1 hour. Let cool completely on a wire rack. Drizzle with Maple-Bourbon Glaze. Garnish with pecans and zest, if desired.

Maple-Bourbon Glaze
MAKES ABOUT 1 CUP

½   (8-ounce) package reduced-fat cream cheese, softened
¼   cup reduced-fat milk
6   tablespoons confectioners' sugar
1   tablespoon maple syrup
1   tablespoon bourbon

1. In a medium bowl, whisk cream cheese until smooth. Gradually add milk, whisking gently until combined. Add confectioners' sugar, maple syrup, and bourbon, whisking until smooth.

Sweet Potato-Sage Scones with Vanilla Bean Maple Glaze

MAKES 8

Scones:
1   large sweet potato
2   cups all-purpose flour
¼   cup sugar
¼   cup chopped fresh sage
1   tablespoon baking powder
1   teaspoon ground cinnamon
½   teaspoon kosher salt
½   teaspoon grated fresh nutmeg
½   cup cold unsalted butter, cubed
1   cup plus 1 tablespoon heavy whipping
     cream, divided
1   large egg

Glaze:
½   cup maple syrup
½   vanilla bean, split lengthwise, seeds
     scraped and reserved
1   cup confectioners' sugar

1. Preheat oven to 400°. Spray an 8-inch round cake pan with baking spray with flour. Line a baking sheet with foil.
2. For scones: Scrub sweet potato, pat dry, and pierce several times with a fork. Bake for 40 minutes. Let cool for 10 minutes. Remove peel. In a medium bowl, mash with a fork. Cover and refrigerate for 20 minutes before incorporating into dough.
3. Increase oven temperature to 425°. In the work bowl of a food processor, combine flour, sugar, sage, baking powder, cinnamon, salt, and nutmeg. Pulse to combine. Add cold butter, and pulse until mixture is crumbly. Transfer mixture to a medium bowl, and fold in mashed sweet potato and 1 cup cream.
4. Turn out dough onto a lightly floured surface, and knead gently, just until dough comes together. Press dough into prepared cake pan. Turn out, and using a sharp knife or bench scraper, cut into 8 wedges. Transfer wedges to prepared baking sheet.
5. Whisk together egg and remaining 1 tablespoon cream. Brush tops with egg wash, and bake until golden brown, 12 to 15 minutes.
6. For glaze: In a small saucepan, heat maple syrup, vanilla bean, and reserved vanilla bean seeds over low heat, cooking until warm and fragrant (do not boil). Remove from heat, and let cool slightly. Strain mixture through a fine-mesh sieve into a bowl, discarding solids. Whisk in confectioners' sugar until smooth. Drizzle over warm scones.

Pumpkin Pie with Coconut Whipped Cream

MAKES 1 (9-INCH) PIE

½   (14.1-ounce) package refrigerated piecrusts
1   (15-ounce) can pumpkin
1⅓   cups coconut milk, divided
¾   cup plus 2 tablespoons sugar, divided
2   large eggs
1½   teaspoons pumpkin pie spice
½   teaspoon kosher salt
⅔   cup heavy whipping cream
Garnish: toasted sweetened flaked coconut

1. Preheat oven to 350°.
2. On a lightly floured surface, roll dough into a 12-inch circle. Press into bottom and up sides of a 9-inch pie plate. Fold edges under, and crimp as desired. Place a piece of parchment paper over crust, letting ends extend over edges of plate. Add pie weights.
3. Bake until lightly browned, about 15 minutes. Carefully remove paper and weights. Let cool completely.
4. In a medium bowl, whisk together pumpkin, 1 cup coconut milk, ¾ cup sugar, eggs, pumpkin pie spice, and salt. Pour mixture into prepared crust.
5. Bake until center is set, 45 to 50 minutes, loosely covering with foil to prevent excess browning, if necessary. Let cool completely on a wire rack.
6. In a medium bowl, beat cream and remaining 2 tablespoons sugar until soft peaks form. Add remaining ⅓ cup coconut milk; beat until stiff peaks form. Top pie with whipped cream, and garnish with coconut, if desired.

Pumpkin Spice Bread

MAKES 1 (10X5-INCH) LOAF

2   cups all-purpose flour
1½   teaspoons baking powder
1   teaspoon salt
1   teaspoon ground cinnamon
½   teaspoon baking soda
½   teaspoon ground allspice
¼   teaspoon ground turmeric
¼   teaspoon Chinese five-spice powder
¼   teaspoon ground ginger
1½   cups canned pumpkin
¾   cup granulated sugar
½   cup firmly packed dark brown sugar
½   cup vegetable oil
¼   cup unsulphured molasses
1   teaspoon vanilla extract
Maple-Ginger Glaze (recipe follows)
Garnish: crystallized ginger

1. Preheat oven to 350°. Spray a 10x5-inch loaf pan with baking spray with flour.
2. In a medium bowl, whisk together flour, baking powder, salt, cinnamon, baking soda, allspice, turmeric, five-spice powder, and ground ginger.
3. In another medium bowl, stir together pumpkin, sugars, oil, molasses, and vanilla. Add flour mixture to pumpkin mixture, stirring to combine. Pour batter into prepared pan.
4. Bake until a wooden pick inserted in center comes out clean, about 1 hour. Let cool in pan for 10 minutes. Remove from pan, and let cool completely on a wire rack.
5. Drizzle bread with Maple-Ginger Glaze. Garnish with crystallized ginger, if desired.

Maple-Ginger Glaze
MAKES ABOUT 1 CUP

1   cup confectioners' sugar
1½   tablespoons water
½   teaspoon grated fresh ginger
¼   teaspoon ground ginger
¼   teaspoon maple flavoring
⅛   teaspoon salt

1. In a small bowl, whisk together confectioners' sugar and 1½ tablespoons water until smooth. Whisk in gingers, maple flavoring, and salt until combined.

BE SURE TO LET BREAD COOL COMPLETELY BEFORE DRIZZLING WITH GLAZE AND SLICING.

Pumpkin Crumble Tart

MAKES ABOUT 8 SERVINGS

Crumble:
- ⅓ cup all-purpose flour
- ⅓ cup granulated sugar
- 3 tablespoons firmly packed light brown sugar
- ¼ teaspoon ground cinnamon
- ⅛ teaspoon salt
- 3 tablespoons cold unsalted butter, cubed
- ½ cup chopped pecans
- ½ (14.1-ounce) package refrigerated piecrusts

Filling:
- 1 (15-ounce) can pumpkin
- 2 large eggs
- ½ cup firmly packed light brown sugar
- ½ cup evaporated whole milk
- 1 teaspoon orange zest
- ½ teaspoon pumpkin pie spice
- ⅛ teaspoon salt
- Apple Cider Syrup (recipe on page 133)

1. For crumble: In a medium bowl, stir together flour, sugars, cinnamon, and salt. Using a pastry blender or 2 forks, cut in butter until mixture is crumbly. Stir in pecans. Cover and refrigerate for 20 minutes.

2. Preheat oven to 375°.

3. On a lightly floured surface, roll dough into a 12-inch circle. Press into bottom and up sides of a 10-inch cast-iron skillet. Fold edges under, and crimp as desired.

4. For filling: In a large bowl, whisk together pumpkin, eggs, brown sugar, milk, zest, pumpkin pie spice, and salt until combined. Pour into prepared crust. Sprinkle crumble over filling.

5. Bake until crust is golden brown and filling is set, about 35 minutes. Let cool completely on a wire rack. Drizzle with Apple Cider Syrup.

Sweet Potato Biscuits

MAKES 10

2½   cups self-rising flour
3   tablespoons sugar
½   cup cold unsalted butter, cubed
¾   cup mashed sweet potato, chilled
½   cup cold whole buttermilk
2   tablespoons unsalted butter, melted
Butter and honey, to serve

1. Preheat oven to 425°. Line a rimmed baking sheet with parchment paper.
2. In a large bowl, stir together flour and sugar. Using a pastry blender or 2 forks, cut in cold butter until mixture is crumbly. Add sweet potato and buttermilk, stirring just until combined.
3. Turn out dough onto a heavily floured surface. Shape dough into a flat log; fold into thirds, letter-style. Roll into a 10x9-inch rectangle. Using a 2½-inch round cutter dipped in flour, cut dough without twisting cutter, rerolling scraps as necessary. Place biscuits 2 inches apart on prepared pan. Brush tops with melted butter. Freeze for 10 minutes.
4. Bake until golden brown and cooked through, about 12 minutes. Serve with butter and honey, if desired.

Spiced Sweet Potato Pie

MAKES 1 (9-INCH) DEEP-DISH PIE

1   (14.1-ounce) package refrigerated piecrusts
1   (15-ounce) can sweet potato purée
2   tablespoons unsalted butter, softened
3   large eggs
2   large egg yolks
⅓   cup firmly packed dark brown sugar
⅓   cup granulated sugar
2   tablespoons bourbon
2   teaspoons vanilla extract
¼   teaspoon ground nutmeg
¼   teaspoon ground ginger
¼   teaspoon ground allspice
Meringue (recipe follows)

1. Preheat oven to 450°.
2. On a lightly floured surface, stack piecrusts, and roll into a 12-inch circle. Press into bottom and up sides of a 9-inch deep-dish pie plate. Fold edges under, and crimp as desired. Using a fork, prick bottom of dough 10 times. Place a piece of parchment paper over crust, letting ends extend over edges of plate. Add pie weights.
3. Bake for 10 minutes. Carefully remove paper and weights, and bake 8 minutes more. Let cool on a wire rack. Reduce oven temperature to 350°. Position rack in bottom third of oven.
4. In a medium bowl, stir together sweet potato and butter until combined. In another medium bowl, whisk together eggs, egg yolks, sugars, bourbon, vanilla, nutmeg, ginger, and allspice. Whisk egg mixture into sweet potato mixture until combined. Pour mixture into prepared crust. Place pie on a rimmed baking sheet.
5. Bake until edges are set, about 45 minutes, covering with foil halfway through baking to prevent excess browning, if necessary. (Center will not be set.) Let cool to room temperature on a wire rack. Spoon Meringue over filling, spreading to seal edges.
6. Bake until Meringue is golden brown, 20 to 25 minutes.

Meringue
MAKES TOPPING FOR 1 (9-INCH) PIE

4   large egg whites, room temperature
¼   teaspoon cream of tartar
⅛   teaspoon salt
¾   cup sugar

1. In the bowl of stand mixer fitted with the whisk attachment, beat egg whites, cream of tartar, and salt at medium-high speed until frothy. Increase mixer speed to high. Gradually add sugar, beating until stiff glossy peaks form, 6 to 8 minutes. Use immediately.

Upside-Down Sweet Potato Cake

MAKES 1 (10-INCH) CAKE

¾   cup cane syrup, divided
2   tablespoons unsalted butter
2½   cups peeled thinly sliced sweet potato
1¾   cups self-rising flour
¾   cup sugar
¼   cup whole milk
10   tablespoons unsalted butter, melted
3   large eggs, lightly beaten
¾   cup sour cream

1. Preheat oven to 350°.
2. In a 10-inch cast-iron skillet, bring ½ cup cane syrup and 2 tablespoons butter to a boil over medium heat; cook for 1 minute. Remove from heat. Layer sweet potato in bottom of skillet, overlapping slightly.
3. In a large bowl, stir together flour and sugar. Add milk, melted butter, eggs, sour cream, and remaining ¼ cup cane syrup. Beat with a mixer at low speed until smooth. Gently spread over sweet potato.
4. Bake until cake is set and golden brown, about 30 minutes. Let stand for 5 minutes. Carefully invert cake onto a flat serving plate.

SPICE-SWIRLED SWEET POTATO BUNDT CAKE

MAKES 8 TO 10 SERVINGS

Cake:
¾ cup unsalted butter, softened
1 (8-ounce) package cream cheese, softened
1⅓ cups granulated sugar, divided
1 cup plus 1 tablespoon firmly packed light brown sugar, divided
4 large eggs
1½ cups peeled grated sweet potato
1 teaspoon vanilla extract
3 cups self-rising flour
1 tablespoon plus 1½ teaspoons pumpkin pie spice, divided

Glaze:
¼ cup firmly packed light brown sugar
3 tablespoons heavy whipping cream, divided
1 tablespoon unsalted butter
1 tablespoon light corn syrup
1 cup confectioners' sugar, sifted
⅛ teaspoon salt

Garnish: chopped toasted pecans

1. Preheat oven to 350°. Spray a 10- to 15-cup Bundt pan with baking spray with flour.
2. For cake: In a large bowl, beat butter and cream cheese with a mixer at medium speed until creamy. Add 1 cup granulated sugar and 1 cup brown sugar; beat until fluffy, 3 to 4 minutes, stopping to scrape sides of bowl. Add eggs, one at a time, beating well after each addition. Add sweet potato and vanilla, beating until combined.
3. In a medium bowl, whisk together flour and 1½ teaspoons pumpkin pie spice. Gradually add flour mixture to sweet potato mixture, beating at low speed just until combined.
4. In a small bowl, stir together remaining ⅓ cup granulated sugar, remaining 1 tablespoon brown sugar, and remaining 1 tablespoon pumpkin pie spice. Spoon one-third of batter into prepared pan, spreading evenly. Sprinkle with half of sugar-spice mixture. Repeat procedure once; top with remaining batter. Tap pan on counter 3 times to release air bubbles.
5. Bake until a wooden pick inserted near center comes out clean, about 45 minutes. Let cool in pan for 10 minutes. Remove from pan, and let cool completely on a wire rack.
6. For glaze: In a small saucepan, bring brown sugar, 2 tablespoons cream, butter, and corn syrup to a simmer over medium heat. Cook, whisking constantly, for 1 minute. Pour into a medium bowl; let cool slightly. Whisk in confectioners' sugar, salt, and remaining 1 tablespoon cream until smooth. Drizzle glaze over cake. Garnish with pecans, if desired.

Pumpkin Upside-Down Cake

MAKES ABOUT 8 SERVINGS

1	cup firmly packed light brown sugar
½	cup unsalted butter
1	tablespoon water
⅔	cup chopped toasted walnuts
½	cup dried cranberries
1	cup canned pumpkin
¾	cup granulated sugar
⅓	cup vegetable oil
2	large eggs
1½	cups all-purpose flour
1½	teaspoons baking powder
1	teaspoon ground cinnamon
¼	teaspoon ground ginger
¼	teaspoon salt
⅛	teaspoon ground cloves

1. Preheat oven to 350°. Line an 8-inch square baking dish with parchment paper. Spray with baking spray with flour.

2. In a small saucepan, cook brown sugar, butter, and 1 tablespoon water over medium-high heat until mixture bubbles, about 4 minutes. Pour sugar mixture into bottom of prepared dish; sprinkle with walnuts and cranberries.

3. In a medium bowl, combine pumpkin, granulated sugar, oil, and eggs, whisking until well blended.

4. In a large bowl, sift together flour, baking powder, cinnamon, ginger, salt, and cloves. Add pumpkin mixture, stirring to combine. Spoon batter over walnuts and cranberries, smoothing top with a spatula.

5. Bake until a wooden pick inserted in center comes out clean, 30 to 40 minutes. Let cool in pan for 5 minutes. Invert pan onto a serving platter. Remove parchment paper, and serve warm.

Nuts & Grains

These hearty harvest favorites anchor
the season's sideboard

CHOCOLATE TART WITH HONEY-GLAZED PECANS

MAKES 1 (9-INCH) TART

2   cups crushed cinnamon graham crackers
½   cup unsalted butter, melted
1¼   cups heavy whipping cream
1   (12-ounce) package semisweet
     chocolate morsels
1   large egg
1   large egg yolk
1   teaspoon vanilla extract
¼   teaspoon kosher salt
Garnish: Honey-Glazed Pecans (recipe follows)

1. Preheat oven to 350°.
2. In a medium bowl, stir together crushed graham crackers and melted butter until well combined. Press into bottom and up sides of a 9-inch removable-bottom tart pan.
3. Bake until golden brown, about 10 minutes. Let cool completely. Reduce oven temperature to 250°.
4. In a medium saucepan, heat cream and chocolate over medium heat, stirring constantly, just until chocolate melts. Remove from heat. In a large bowl, gently whisk together egg and egg yolk. Gradually add chocolate, whisking constantly. Whisk in vanilla and salt. Pour filling into cooled crust.
5. Bake until center is set, 30 to 35 minutes. Let cool completely on a wire rack. Refrigerate until chilled, at least 3 hours. Garnish with Honey-Glazed Pecans, if desired. Let cool completely before slicing. Cover and refrigerate for up to 3 days.

HONEY-GLAZED PECANS

MAKES 2 CUPS

2   cups pecan halves
1   teaspoon canola oil
¼   teaspoon kosher salt
⅓   cup honey

1. Preheat oven to 350°.
2. On a rimmed baking sheet, stir together pecans, oil, and salt until combined. Bake for 7 minutes.
3. In a medium saucepan, bring honey to a boil over medium-high heat. Add pecans, stirring to coat. Cook 1 minute more; remove from heat. Let cool slightly.

Pecan Crumble Coffee Cake

MAKES 8 SERVINGS

¼ cup butter, softened
½ (8-ounce) package cream cheese, softened
¾ cup sugar
1 large egg
1 cup all-purpose flour
½ teaspoon baking powder
¼ teaspoon salt
¼ cup whole milk
½ teaspoon vanilla extract
1 teaspoon cinnamon
Crumb Topping (recipe follows)

1. Preheat oven to 350°. Spray a 9-inch cast-iron wedge pan with baking spray with flour.
2. In a large bowl, beat butter and cream cheese with a mixer at medium speed until creamy. Gradually add sugar, beating until fluffy, 3 to 4 minutes. Add egg, beating just until combined.
3. In a medium bowl, whisk together flour, baking powder, and salt. Gradually add flour mixture to butter mixture alternately with milk, beginning and ending with flour mixture, beating just until combined after each addition. Beat in vanilla. Spoon ⅓ cup batter into a small bowl, and stir in cinnamon. Pour remaining batter into wedges. Top each wedge with cinnamon batter, and swirl with a knife. Sprinkle with Crumb Topping.
4. Bake until a wooden pick inserted in center comes out clean, 20 to 25 minutes. Let cool for 20 minutes.

CRUMB TOPPING
MAKES ⅔ CUP

2 tablespoons sugar
2 tablespoons all-purpose flour
2 tablespoons cold unsalted butter
¼ cup finely chopped pecans

1. In a small bowl, combine sugar and flour. Cut in butter until mixture is crumbly. Stir in pecans. Refrigerate until ready to use.

Butter Pecan Angel Food Cake

MAKES 8 TO 10 SERVINGS

1½ cups confectioners' sugar
1 cup cake flour
¾ teaspoon salt
¾ cup finely ground pecans
12 egg whites, room temperature
1½ teaspoons cream of tartar
2 tablespoons butter flavoring
1 tablespoon vanilla, butter, and nut flavoring*
1 tablespoon vanilla extract
1 cup granulated sugar
Brown Butter Glaze (recipe follows)
Garnish: chopped toasted pecans

1. Preheat oven to 375°.
2. In a medium bowl, sift together confectioners'
sugar, flour, and salt. Stir in pecans. Set aside.
3. In a large bowl, beat egg whites, cream of tartar,
flavorings, and vanilla with a mixer at high speed
until frothy. Gradually add granulated sugar,
beating until stiff peaks form. Gently fold flour
mixture into egg white mixture in thirds, folding
until combined. Spoon batter into an ungreased
10-cup Bundt pan.
4. Bake until golden brown, about 40 minutes.
Invert pan onto the top of a bottle. Let cool
completely.
5. Once cooled, remove cake from pan. Pour
Brown Butter Glaze over cake. Garnish with
pecans, if desired.

*We used McCormick Imitation Vanilla, Butter &
Nut Flavor.*

Brown Butter Glaze
MAKES ABOUT 1 CUP

1 cup confectioners' sugar, sifted
⅛ teaspoon salt
10 tablespoons unsalted butter, cubed

1. In a medium bowl, stir together confectioners'
sugar and salt; set aside.
2. In a medium saucepan, melt butter over
medium heat. Cook until butter turns a
medium-brown color and has a nutty aroma,
about 10 minutes. Strain butter through a
fine-mesh sieve over sugar mixture; whisk until
smooth.

Butterscotch-Pecan Personal Pan Cookies

MAKES 12 SERVINGS

1   cup unsalted butter, softened
1½   cups firmly packed light brown sugar
1   cup granulated sugar
3   large eggs
2   teaspoons vanilla extract
3   cups all-purpose flour
1½   teaspoons baking powder
1½   teaspoons kosher salt
1   (11-ounce) package butterscotch morsels
1   cup chopped pecans
Vanilla ice cream, to serve

1. Preheat oven to 375°.
2. In a large bowl, beat butter and sugars with a mixer at high speed until fluffy, 3 to 4 minutes, stopping to scrape sides of bowl. Add eggs, one at a time, beating well after each addition. Beat in vanilla.
3. In a small bowl, whisk together flour, baking powder, and salt. Gradually add flour mixture to butter mixture, beating just until combined. Stir in butterscotch and pecans. Divide batter among 12 (4½-inch) cast-iron skillets.
4. Bake until lightly browned, about 30 minutes. Let cool for 10 minutes. Serve in skillets with vanilla ice cream, if desired.

Oatmeal-Pecan Fig Bars

MAKES ABOUT 16

3   cups chopped dried figs
1   cup water
½   cup dry red wine
¼   cup granulated sugar
½   teaspoon orange zest
⅛   teaspoon kosher salt
¾   cup unsalted butter
1   cup firmly packed light brown sugar
1¾   cups all-purpose flour
1¼   teaspoons kosher salt
½   teaspoon baking soda
1   cup old-fashioned oats
½   cup finely chopped pecans

1. Preheat oven to 375°. Spray a 13x9-inch baking dish with cooking spray.
2. In a medium saucepan, bring figs, 1 cup water, wine, granulated sugar, zest, and salt to a boil over medium-high heat, stirring constantly. Reduce heat to medium-low. Cook, stirring occasionally, until mixture thickens and reduces to 2½ cups, about 10 minutes. Remove from heat, and let cool completely.

3. In a large bowl, beat butter and brown sugar with a mixer at medium speed until fluffy, 3 to 4 minutes, stopping to scrape sides of bowl. In a medium bowl, stir together flour, salt, and baking soda. Gradually add flour mixture to butter mixture, beating to combine. (Mixture will be crumbly.) Gradually add oats and pecans, beating just until combined.
4. Using the bottom of a measuring cup, firmly press half of crust mixture into bottom of prepared pan. Gently spread fig mixture over crust. Sprinkle remaining crust mixture over fig layer, pressing lightly.
5. Bake until golden brown, 25 to 30 minutes. Let cool slightly. Cut into bars. Cover and refrigerate for up to 3 days.

Chocolate-Butterscotch Crispy Bars

MAKES 10 TO 12 SERVINGS

1 cup honey
½ cup sugar
1¼ cups crunchy peanut butter
6 cups crisp rice cereal
1 (12-ounce) package semisweet chocolate morsels
1 (12-ounce) package butterscotch morsels
½ cup chopped honey-roasted peanuts

1. Spray a 13x9-inch baking pan with cooking spray.
2. In a large saucepan, bring honey and sugar to a boil over medium-high heat. Remove from heat. Add peanut butter, stirring until combined. Add cereal, stirring until evenly coated. (Mixture will be thick.) Press cereal mixture into prepared pan.
3. In a medium microwave-safe bowl, place chocolate and butterscotch. Microwave on high in 30-second intervals, stirring between each, until melted and smooth. Spread chocolate mixture in an even layer over cereal mixture. Top with peanuts. Let cool until chocolate hardens; cut into squares. Store in an airtight container for up to 3 days.

Pecan Praline Cookies

MAKES ABOUT 60

1 cup unsalted butter, softened
⅔ cup granulated sugar
½ cup confectioners' sugar
2 large eggs
2 teaspoons vanilla extract
3 cups all-purpose flour
1 teaspoon baking powder
½ teaspoon salt
3 tablespoons heavy whipping cream
1 (11-ounce) package caramel bits
¼ cup water
60 praline pecans
Sea salt (optional)

1. In a large bowl, beat butter and sugars with a mixer at medium-high speed until fluffy, 3 to 4 minutes. Add eggs, one at a time, beating well after each addition. Beat in vanilla.
2. In a medium bowl, sift together flour, baking powder, and salt. Gradually add flour mixture to butter mixture, beating until smooth. Add cream, beating to combine. Shape dough into a disk, and wrap in plastic wrap. Refrigerate for at least 1 hour.

3. Preheat oven to 350°. Line baking sheets with parchment paper.
4. On a lightly floured surface, roll dough to ¼-inch thickness. Using a 2-inch fluted round cutter, cut dough, rerolling scraps no more than twice. Place on prepared pans.
5. Bake until edges are lightly browned, about 10 minutes. Let cool on pans for 2 minutes. Remove from pans, and let cool completely on wire racks.
6. In a small saucepan, cook caramel bits and ¼ cup water over medium heat, whisking often, until bits are melted and mixture is smooth. Let cool to room temperature.
7. Spread about ½ teaspoon caramel mixture on center of each cookie. Press a praline pecan into caramel. Sprinkle with sea salt, if desired. Place cookies on parchment paper to dry, about 1 hour. Store in an airtight container at room temperature for up to 1 week.

White Chocolate and Toasted Nut Tart

MAKES 1 (9-INCH) TART

1   (12-ounce) jar prepared caramel
     topping, divided
Best Tart Shell (recipe follows)
3   (4-ounce) bars white chocolate, chopped
¼   cup plus 3 tablespoons heavy
     whipping cream
¼   cup butter
2   tablespoons light corn syrup
1   (11.5-ounce) can mixed nuts, toasted
¼   cup walnuts, toasted
¼   cup macadamia nuts, toasted

1. Pour half of prepared caramel topping into
bottom of Best Tart Shell, spreading to cover
entire surface. Refrigerate for 30 minutes.
2. Place white chocolate in a medium bowl. In a
medium saucepan, bring cream, butter, and corn
syrup to a boil over high heat. Pour mixture over
chopped chocolate, whisking until melted and
smooth. Pour chocolate mixture over caramel in
prepared tart shell. Refrigerate until set, about
2 hours.
3. In a medium bowl, combine nuts and remaining
caramel topping. Gently spoon nut mixture on
top of tart. Remove sides of tart pan before
serving. Store, covered, at room temperature for
up to 2 days.

Best Tart Shell
MAKES 1 (11X9-INCH) TART SHELL

1½   cups all-purpose flour
¼   cup confectioners' sugar
¼   teaspoon salt
½   cup unsalted butter, softened
1   large egg yolk
1   tablespoon heavy whipping cream

1. In the work bowl of a food processor, pulse
together flour, confectioners' sugar, and salt
until combined. Add butter, egg yolk, and
cream, pulsing until mixture comes together.
Shape into a disk, and wrap in plastic wrap.
Refrigerate for 2 hours.
2. Preheat oven to 350°.
3. On a lightly floured surface, roll dough into
a 13x11-inch rectangle, ¼ inch thick. Press
dough into bottom and up sides of an
11x9-inch tart pan, trimming dough if
necessary. Place a piece of parchment paper
over tart shell, letting ends extend over edges
of pan. Add pie weights.
4. Bake until golden brown, about
30 minutes. Carefully remove paper and
weights. Let cool for 30 minutes.

White Chocolate Cranberry Toffee

MAKES ABOUT 54 PIECES

54   saltine crackers
1   cup butter
1   cup firmly packed light brown sugar
1   (14-ounce) can sweetened condensed milk
6   (1-ounce) squares white chocolate, finely chopped
1   cup chopped pecans
½   cup chopped sweetened dried cranberries

1. Preheat oven to 425°. Line a 15x10-inch jelly-roll pan with heavy-duty foil. Spray foil with cooking spray.
2. Arrange crackers in an even layer on prepared pan.
3. In a medium saucepan, bring butter and brown sugar to a boil over medium-high heat. Cook for 2 minutes. Remove from heat, and stir in condensed milk. Pour mixture over crackers.
4. Bake for 10 minutes. Sprinkle with chopped chocolate. Let stand for 1 to 2 minutes to soften. Using a small offset spatula, spread softened chocolate over baked toffee. Sprinkle with pecans and cranberries. Let cool completely.
5. Break toffee into cracker-size pieces. Store in an airtight container for up to 5 days.

BUTTERSCOTCH-WALNUT BLONDIES

MAKES ABOUT 9

1   cup unsalted butter, melted and slightly cooled
1½   cups firmly packed light brown sugar
2   large eggs
2   teaspoons vanilla extract
2   cups all-purpose flour
1   teaspoon baking powder
1   teaspoon kosher salt
¾   cup butterscotch morsels
¾   cup chopped walnuts

1. Preheat oven to 350°. Spray an 8-inch square baking pan with baking spray with flour.
2. In a medium bowl, whisk together melted butter and brown sugar until smooth. Whisk in eggs and vanilla.
3. In another medium bowl, whisk together flour, baking powder, and salt. Gradually add egg mixture to flour mixture, stirring to combine. Gently stir in butterscotch and walnuts. Spread batter in prepared pan, smoothing top with an offset spatula.
4. Bake until golden brown and a wooden pick inserted in center comes out clean, about 20 minutes. Let cool completely in pan.

Multigrain Bread

MAKES 2 LOAVES

4 to 5 cups bread flour, divided
1 cup whole wheat flour
¾ cup finely chopped pecans
½ cup plus 2 tablespoons oats, divided
½ cup plus 2 tablespoons roasted sunflower seed kernels, divided
½ cup barley flour
¼ cup wheat germ
¼ cup unprocessed wheat bran
2½ teaspoons salt
1 cup warm water (105° to 110°)
1 (0.25-ounce) package active dry yeast
¼ cup sugar
2 cups warm whole milk (105° to 110°)
¼ cup vegetable oil
¼ cup honey
1 large egg white, lightly beaten

1. In a large bowl, combine 1 cup bread flour, whole wheat flour, pecans, ½ cup oats, ½ cup sunflower seed kernels, barley flour, wheat germ, wheat bran, and salt.

2. In a medium bowl, stir together 1 cup warm water, yeast, and sugar. Let stand until mixture is foamy, about 5 minutes. Stir in warm milk, oil, and honey.

3. Add yeast mixture to flour mixture, and beat with a mixer at low speed until smooth. Gradually beat in enough remaining bread flour to make a soft dough.

4. Turn out dough onto a lightly floured surface, and knead until dough is smooth and elastic, about 5 minutes. Spray a large bowl with cooking spray. Place dough in bowl, turning to grease top. Cover and let rise in a warm, draft-free place (75°) until doubled in size, about 1 hour.

5. Lightly spray 2 baking sheets with cooking spray.

6. Divide dough into 2 equal portions. Shape each portion into 2 (15-inch) ropes. Pinch 2 ropes together at one end to seal, and twist ropes together. Pinch ends together to seal. Shape twisted ropes into a round loaf, pinching ends together to seal. Repeat procedure with remaining 2 bread ropes. Place 1 loaf on each prepared pan. Cover and let rise in a warm, draft-free place (75°) until doubled in size, about 1 hour.

7. Preheat oven to 350°.

8. Gently brush loaves with egg white, and sprinkle with remaining 2 tablespoons oats and remaining 2 tablespoons sunflower seed kernels.

9. Bake for 40 minutes, covering with foil to prevent excess browning, if necessary. Let cool for 30 minutes before slicing. Store in an airtight container for up to 5 days.

CLASSIC PECAN PIE

MAKES 1 (9-INCH) PIE

Crust:
1¼ cups all-purpose flour
1 teaspoon kosher salt
1 teaspoon sugar
½ cup cold unsalted butter, cubed
3 to 4 tablespoons whole buttermilk, chilled

Filling:
3 large eggs
1 cup firmly packed light brown sugar
¾ cup light corn syrup
½ cup melted unsalted butter, room temperature
1 teaspoon kosher salt
1 teaspoon vanilla extract
2 cups pecan halves

1. Preheat oven to 350°.
2. For crust: In a medium bowl, stir together flour, salt, and sugar. Using a pastry blender, cut in butter until mixture is crumbly. Add buttermilk, 1 tablespoon at a time, stirring to form a dough. Shape dough into a disk, and wrap tightly in plastic wrap. Refrigerate until firm, at least 30 minutes.
3. On a lightly floured surface, roll dough to ⅛-inch thickness. Transfer to a 9-inch pie plate, pressing into bottom and up sides. Fold edges under, and crimp as desired.
4. For filling: In a medium bowl, stir together eggs, brown sugar, corn syrup, melted butter, salt, and vanilla; gently stir in pecans. Pour mixture into prepared crust.
5. Bake for 30 minutes. Cover loosely with foil, and bake until center is set, about 20 minutes more. Let cool completely before slicing.

Brown Butter-Pecan Tassies

MAKES ABOUT 24

Dough:
½   cup Easy Brown Butter, softened (recipe follows)
½   (8-ounce) package cream cheese, softened
1¼   cups all-purpose flour
1   tablespoon sugar
¾   teaspoon salt

Filling:
½   cup firmly packed light brown sugar
1   tablespoon Easy Brown Butter, melted
1   tablespoon corn syrup
1   tablespoon cane syrup
1   teaspoon vanilla extract
1   large egg, lightly beaten
⅛   teaspoon salt
⅔   cup chopped pecans
24   pecan halves

1. For dough: In a large bowl, beat softened Easy Brown Butter and cream cheese with a mixer at medium speed until smooth. Gradually add flour, sugar, and salt, beating at low speed until a firm dough forms, stopping to scrape sides of bowl. Turn out dough onto a lightly floured surface, and shape into a disk. Cover with plastic wrap, and refrigerate for 30 minutes.
2. Preheat oven to 350°. Spray 24 miniature muffin cups with baking spray with flour.
3. Scoop 24 heaping tablespoonfuls of dough, and roll into balls. Place 1 ball in each prepared muffin cup, pressing into bottom and up sides.
4. For filling: In a small bowl, whisk together brown sugar, melted Easy Brown Butter, corn syrup, cane syrup, vanilla, egg, and salt.
5. Sprinkle ½ teaspoon chopped pecans in each muffin cup. Spoon 1½ teaspoons filling over pecans. Top with pecan halves.
6. Bake until set and lightly browned, about 20 minutes. Run a knife around edges to loosen; gently remove from muffin cups. Let cool completely on a wire rack. Store in an airtight container for up to 3 days.

Easy Brown Butter
MAKES ABOUT ¾ CUP

¾   cup unsalted butter

1. In a medium saucepan, melt butter over medium heat. Cook until butter turns a medium-brown color and has a nutty aroma, about 10 minutes. Strain through a fine-mesh sieve into a small bowl. Cover and refrigerate for 45 minutes, stirring twice.

Pecan Pie Cupcakes

MAKES 12

½ cup unsalted butter, softened
¾ cup firmly packed dark brown sugar
2 large eggs, room temperature
1 cup all-purpose flour
1 teaspoon baking powder
¼ teaspoon salt
½ cup whole milk, room temperature
⅔ cup chopped pecans, toasted
1 teaspoon vanilla extract
Brown Sugar Buttercream Frosting
   (recipe follows)
Garnish: chopped toasted pecans

1. Preheat oven to 350°. Line 12 muffin cups with paper liners.
2. In a large bowl, beat butter and brown sugar with a mixer at medium speed until fluffy, 3 to 4 minutes, stopping to scrape sides of bowl. Add eggs, one at a time, beating well after each addition.
3. In a medium bowl, sift together flour, baking powder, and salt. Gradually add flour mixture to butter mixture alternately with milk, beginning and ending with flour mixture, beating just until combined after each addition. Fold in pecans and vanilla. Divide batter among prepared muffin cups.
4. Bake until a wooden pick inserted in center comes out clean, 18 to 20 minutes. Let cool in pan for 5 minutes. Remove from pan, and let cool completely on a wire rack.
5. Spread Brown Sugar Buttercream Frosting on cupcakes. Garnish with pecans, if desired.

Brown Sugar Buttercream Frosting
MAKES ABOUT 1¾ CUPS

¼ cup firmly packed dark brown sugar
2 tablespoons water
¼ teaspoon salt
½ cup plus 2 tablespoons unsalted butter, softened and divided
3½ cups confectioners' sugar
2 to 3 tablespoons whole milk

1. In a small saucepan, bring brown sugar, 2 tablespoons water, and salt to a boil over medium-high heat. Cook, stirring constantly, until sugar is dissolved, about 1 minute. Remove from heat; stir in 2 tablespoons butter. Let cool completely.
2. In a large bowl, beat cooled brown sugar mixture and remaining ½ cup butter with a mixer at medium speed until creamy. Beat in confectioners' sugar and enough milk to reach a spreadable consistency.

Autumn Spices

Let cinnamon, nutmeg, cardamom, and allspice warm your kitchen

PUMPKIN SPICE SKILLET COOKIE

MAKES ABOUT 4 SERVINGS

½   cup unsalted butter, softened
¾   cup firmly packed light brown sugar
1   large egg
1   teaspoon vanilla extract
¾   cup all-purpose flour
1   teaspoon Homemade Pumpkin Spice (recipe on page 133)
¾   teaspoon baking powder
¼   teaspoon kosher salt
½   cup plus 2 tablespoons old-fashioned oats, divided
½   cup sweetened dried cranberries
⅓   cup butterscotch morsels
Garnish: butterscotch morsels

1. Preheat oven to 325°. Spray an 8-inch cast-iron skillet with baking spray with flour.
2. In a large bowl, beat butter and brown sugar with a mixer at medium speed until fluffy, 3 to 4 minutes, stopping to scrape sides of bowl. Add egg and vanilla; beat until combined.
3. In a small bowl, whisk together flour, Homemade Pumpkin Spice, baking powder, and salt. Reduce mixer speed to low; add flour mixture to butter mixture, beating just until combined. Stir in ½ cup oats. Press half of dough into bottom of prepared skillet. Sprinkle with half of cranberries and half of butterscotch. Top with tablespoonfuls of remaining dough. Sprinkle with remaining 2 tablespoons oats, remaining cranberries, and remaining butterscotch.
4. Bake until golden brown, about 45 minutes, loosely covering with foil to prevent excess browning, if necessary. Let cool for 15 minutes. Garnish with butterscotch, if desired.

PEAR CHAI SPICED SCONES WITH SPICED PEAR SYRUP

MAKES 8

Scones:
2   cups all-purpose flour
¼   cup sugar
1   tablespoon baking powder
2   teaspoons kosher salt
1   teaspoon ground cinnamon
1   teaspoon ground ginger
½   teaspoon grated fresh nutmeg
¼   teaspoon ground cardamom
¼   teaspoon ground black pepper
5   tablespoons cold unsalted butter, cubed
2   small pears, chopped
1   cup plus 1 teaspoon heavy whipping cream, divided
1   large egg

Spiced Pear Syrup:
¼   cup water
¼   cup sugar
1   pear, sliced
1   cinnamon stick
1   star anise

Pear Glaze:
2   tablespoons Spiced Pear Syrup
½   cup confectioners' sugar

1. Preheat oven to 425°. Spray an 8-inch round cake pan with baking spray with flour. Line a baking sheet with parchment paper.

2. For scones: In the work bowl of a food processor, combine flour, sugar, baking powder, salt, cinnamon, ginger, nutmeg, cardamom, and pepper. Pulse to combine. Add cold butter, and pulse until mixture is crumbly.

3. Transfer dough to a large bowl, and fold in pears and 1 cup cream, stirring until combined. Turn out dough onto a lightly floured surface, and knead briefly, just until dough comes together. Press dough into prepared cake pan. Turn out, and using a sharp knife or bench scraper, cut into 8 wedges. Transfer wedges to prepared baking sheet. In a small bowl, whisk together egg and remaining 1 teaspoon cream. Brush tops of wedges with egg wash.

4. Bake until golden brown, 12 to 15 minutes.

5. For syrup: In a small saucepan, bring ¼ cup water, sugar, pears, cinnamon stick, and star anise to a boil over medium-high heat, stirring occasionally, until sugar is dissolved. Remove from heat, and let cool completely. When cool, strain through a fine-mesh sieve into a bowl, discarding solids.

6. For glaze: Whisk together Spiced Pear Syrup and confectioners' sugar until smooth. Drizzle over warm scones.

Orange-Cardamom Bread

MAKES 2 (8X4-INCH) LOAVES

2½ cups sugar
1½ cups whole milk
1 cup vegetable oil
3 large eggs
2 tablespoons orange zest
1½ teaspoons vanilla extract
¼ teaspoon ground cardamom
3 cups all-purpose flour
1½ teaspoons salt
1½ teaspoons baking powder
Orange Glaze (recipe follows)

1. Preheat oven to 350°. Spray 2 (8x4-inch) loaf pans with baking spray with flour.
2. In a large bowl, beat sugar, milk, oil, eggs, zest, vanilla, and cardamom with a mixer at medium speed until well combined. In a medium bowl, sift together flour, salt, and baking powder. Gradually add flour mixture to sugar mixture, beating until smooth. Divide batter between prepared pans.
3. Bake for 30 minutes. Loosely cover with foil, and bake until a wooden pick inserted in center comes out clean, about 30 minutes more. Let cool in pans for 10 minutes. Remove from pans, and let cool completely on a wire rack. Drizzle with Orange Glaze.

Orange Glaze
MAKES ABOUT 1⅓ CUPS

2 cups confectioners' sugar
1 teaspoon orange zest
⅓ cup fresh orange juice

1. In a medium bowl, stir together all ingredients until smooth.

CARROT CAKE

MAKES 1 (9-INCH) CAKE

3   cups all-purpose flour
2½   cups sugar
1   cup golden raisins
¾   cup chopped walnuts
1   tablespoon ground cinnamon
2   teaspoons baking powder
2   teaspoons baking soda
1½   teaspoons salt
1   teaspoon ground ginger
1   teaspoon ground nutmeg
4   cups finely grated carrot
    (about 5 large carrots)
2   (8-ounce) cans crushed pineapple, drained
4   large eggs, lightly beaten
1   cup canola oil
2   teaspoons vanilla extract
Cream Cheese Frosting (recipe follows)

1. Preheat oven to 350°. Spray 3 (9-inch) round cake pans with baking spray with flour. Line bottom of pans with parchment paper, and spray pans again.

2. In a large bowl, stir together flour, sugar, raisins, walnuts, cinnamon, baking powder, baking soda, salt, ginger, and nutmeg. Add carrot, pineapple, eggs, oil, and vanilla; stir until well combined. Divide batter among prepared pans.

3. Bake until a wooden pick inserted in center comes out clean, about 25 minutes. Let cool in pans for 10 minutes. Remove from pans, and let cool completely on wire racks.

4. Spread Cream Cheese Frosting between layers and on top and sides of cake.

CREAM CHEESE FROSTING

MAKES ABOUT 6 CUPS

2   (8-ounce) packages cream cheese, softened
1   cup unsalted butter, softened
1   tablespoon vanilla extract
1   (2-pound) package confectioners' sugar

1. In a large bowl, beat cream cheese and butter with a mixer at medium speed until smooth. Beat in vanilla. Gradually add confectioners' sugar, beating until smooth.

CINNAMON ROLL CAKE

MAKES 6 TO 8 SERVINGS

Streusel:
⅓ cup firmly packed light brown sugar
⅓ cup finely chopped pecans
1 tablespoon ground cinnamon
¼ teaspoon kosher salt

Cake:
½ cup unsalted butter, softened
1½ cups sugar
3 large eggs
2 cups all-purpose flour
1 teaspoon ground cinnamon
1 teaspoon baking powder
½ teaspoon baking soda
½ teaspoon kosher salt
¾ cup whole buttermilk
½ cup sour cream
2 teaspoons vanilla extract
Cream Cheese Glaze (recipe follows)
Garnish: chopped pecans

1. Preheat oven to 350°. Spray a Nordic Ware Cinnamon Bun Pull-Apart Cake Pan with baking spray with flour.
2. For streusel: In a small bowl, stir together brown sugar, pecans, cinnamon, and salt. Set aside.
3. For cake: In a large bowl, beat butter and sugar with a mixer at medium speed until fluffy, 3 to 4 minutes, stopping to scrape sides of bowl. Add eggs, one at a time, beating well after each addition. In a medium bowl, stir together flour, cinnamon, baking powder, baking soda, and salt. In a small bowl, stir together buttermilk and sour cream. With mixer on low speed, gradually add flour mixture to butter mixture alternately with buttermilk mixture, beginning and ending with flour mixture, beating just until combined after each addition. Beat in vanilla.
4. Spoon half of batter into prepared pan, smoothing with an offset spatula. Sprinkle with streusel mixture; top with remaining batter. Using a knife, pull blade back and forth through batter to swirl streusel layer. Smooth top with an offset spatula.
5. Bake until a wooden pick inserted in center comes out clean, 35 to 40 minutes. Let cool in pan for 10 minutes. Remove from pan, and let cool completely on a wire rack. Drizzle with Cream Cheese Glaze, and garnish with pecans, if desired.

CREAM CHEESE GLAZE

MAKES ABOUT 1 CUP

2 ounces cream cheese, softened
2 tablespoons unsalted butter, softened
1 cup confectioners' sugar
2 tablespoons whole milk
½ teaspoon vanilla extract

1. In a medium bowl, whisk together cream cheese and butter until smooth. Add confectioners' sugar, milk, and vanilla, stirring until smooth.

Spice Cookies with Orange Marmalade

MAKES ABOUT 16 SANDWICH COOKIES

¾ cup unsalted butter, softened
½ cup confectioners' sugar, plus more for dusting
1 tablespoon orange zest
½ teaspoon vanilla extract
1½ cups all-purpose flour
1 teaspoon ground cinnamon
½ teaspoon ground nutmeg
¼ teaspoon ground cloves
¼ teaspoon salt
2 tablespoons granulated sugar
2 cups prepared orange marmalade

1. In a large bowl, beat butter, confectioners' sugar, zest, and vanilla with a mixer at medium speed until creamy, 3 to 4 minutes. In a medium bowl, whisk together flour, cinnamon, nutmeg, cloves, and salt. Gradually add flour mixture to butter mixture, beating until combined.
2. Divide dough in half, and wrap each half in plastic wrap. Refrigerate for at least 2 hours or overnight. Remove dough from refrigerator 15 minutes before using.
3. Preheat oven to 350°. Line 2 baking sheets with parchment paper.
4. On a lightly floured surface, roll half of dough to ¼-inch thickness. Using a 2-inch fluted square cutter, cut dough, rerolling scraps once. Repeat process with remaining dough. Using a ¾-inch fluted round cutter, cut centers from half of cookies. Place cookies about 1 inch apart on prepared pans, and sprinkle with granulated sugar.
5. Bake until edges of cookies are lightly browned, 10 to 12 minutes. Let cool on pans for 1 minute. Remove from pans, and let cool completely on wire racks.
6. Dust cookies with cutouts with confectioners' sugar. Spread about 1 teaspoon marmalade on flat side of all solid cookies. Place cookies with cutouts, flat side down, on top of marmalade. Store in an airtight container for up to 5 days.

FILL THESE SANDWICH
COOKIES WITH YOUR
FAVORITE FALL PRESERVES.

SPICE CAKE

MAKES 1 (9-INCH) CAKE

1½   cups unsalted butter, softened
3   cups sugar
2   tablespoons light molasses
6   large eggs, room temperature
3   cups cake flour
1   cup finely ground toasted pecans
2   tablespoons ground cinnamon
2   teaspoons ground allspice
1¼   teaspoons baking soda
1   teaspoon ground nutmeg
¼   teaspoon kosher salt
1   cup sour cream, room temperature
1   tablespoon grated fresh ginger
1   tablespoon vanilla extract
Spice Cake Icing (recipe follows)
2   cups chopped toasted pecans

1. Preheat oven to 350°. Spray 3 (9-inch) round cake pans with baking spray with flour.
2. In a large bowl, beat butter and sugar with a mixer at medium speed until fluffy, 3 to 4 minutes. Add molasses, and beat until combined. Add eggs, one at a time, beating well after each addition. In a medium bowl, whisk together flour, ground pecans, cinnamon, allspice, baking soda, nutmeg, and salt. Gradually add flour mixture to butter mixture alternately with sour cream, beginning and ending with flour mixture, beating just until combined after each addition. Beat in ginger and vanilla. Spoon batter into prepared pans.

3. Bake until a wooden pick inserted in center comes out clean, 35 to 40 minutes. Let cool in pans for 10 minutes. Remove from pans, and let cool completely on wire racks.
4. Spread Spice Cake Icing between layers and on top and sides of cake. Press chopped pecans up sides of cake as desired.

SPICE CAKE ICING

MAKES ABOUT 4½ CUPS

1½   cups unsalted butter, softened
3   (8-ounce) packages cream cheese, softened
7   cups confectioners' sugar
1   tablespoon vanilla extract
1   teaspoon kosher salt

1. In a large bowl, beat butter and cream cheese with a mixer at medium-high speed until creamy, about 5 minutes. Reduce mixer speed to low. Add confectioners' sugar, vanilla, and salt, beating until combined, about 6 minutes.

CINNAMON SWIRLS

MAKES ABOUT 36

1   cup unsalted butter, softened
½   cup granulated sugar
2   large eggs
1   teaspoon vanilla extract
3   cups all-purpose flour
2   teaspoons baking powder
2   tablespoons plus 1 teaspoon ground
    cinnamon, divided
½   teaspoon salt
1   cup firmly packed light brown sugar
2½ cups confectioners' sugar
4 to 5 tablespoons whole milk

1. In a large bowl, beat butter and granulated sugar with a mixer at medium speed until creamy, 3 to 4 minutes. Add eggs, one at a time, beating well after each addition. Beat in vanilla. In a medium bowl, whisk together flour, baking powder, 1 teaspoon cinnamon, and salt. Gradually add flour mixture to butter mixture, beating until combined. Shape dough into a disk, and wrap in plastic wrap. Refrigerate for at least 2 hours.

2. In a small bowl, combine brown sugar and remaining 2 tablespoons cinnamon.

3. On a lightly floured surface, roll dough to ¼-inch thickness. Transfer dough to a piece of parchment paper. Sprinkle brown sugar mixture onto dough, and lightly press in place. Starting at one long side, roll up dough, jelly-roll style. Wrap log in plastic wrap, and refrigerate for 2 hours.

4. Preheat oven to 350°. Line 2 baking sheets with parchment paper.

5. Unwrap dough. Cut into ¼-inch-thick slices. Place 2 inches apart on prepared pans.

6. Bake until golden, 10 to 12 minutes. Let cool on pans for 5 minutes. Remove from pans, and let cool completely on wire racks.

7. In a small bowl, stir together confectioners' sugar and enough milk until a smooth consistency is reached. Drizzle over cooled cookies.

Spiced Chocolate Chunk Cookies

MAKES ABOUT 24

1¾ cups white whole wheat flour
¾ teaspoon ground cinnamon
½ teaspoon ground ginger
½ teaspoon baking soda
¼ teaspoon ground allspice
⅛ teaspoon ground cloves
14 tablespoons unsalted butter, softened and divided
¾ cup firmly packed dark brown sugar
½ cup granulated sugar
2 teaspoons vanilla extract
1 teaspoon kosher salt
1 large egg
1 large egg yolk
1 cup semisweet chocolate chunks
½ cup finely chopped toasted pecans

1. Preheat oven to 375°. Line 2 baking sheets with parchment paper.

2. In a medium bowl, whisk together flour, cinnamon, ginger, baking soda, allspice, and cloves; set aside.

3. In a small skillet, melt 10 tablespoons butter over medium-high heat. Cook until butter is golden brown, 3 to 4 minutes. Transfer to a large bowl. Add remaining 4 tablespoons butter, and stir until melted. Add sugars, vanilla, and salt, stirring to combine. Add egg and egg yolk, whisking until well combined, 3 to 4 minutes.

4. Add flour mixture to butter mixture, stirring until well combined. Add chocolate and pecans, stirring just until combined. Scoop dough by heaping tablespoonfuls, and roll into balls. Place at least 2 inches apart on prepared pans.

5. Bake until edges are golden brown and cookies are puffy, 8 to 14 minutes. Remove from pans, and let cool completely on a wire rack.

BAKED PUMPKIN SPICE DOUGHNUTS

MAKES ABOUT 18

1   (0.25-ounce) package active dry yeast
¼   cup warm water (105° to 110°)
5   cups all-purpose flour, divided
1¼   cups warm half-and-half (105° to 110°)
1   cup firmly packed light brown sugar
½   cup unsalted butter, softened
1   large egg
1   teaspoon salt
1   teaspoon cinnamon
1   teaspoon vanilla extract
½   cup unsalted butter, melted
Cane Syrup Glaze (recipe follows)
½   cup toasted pecans, chopped

1. In a small bowl, stir together yeast and ¼ cup warm water. Let stand until mixture is foamy, about 5 minutes.
2. In the bowl of a stand mixer fitted with the paddle attachment, beat yeast mixture, 3½ cups flour, warm half-and-half, brown sugar, softened butter, egg, salt, cinnamon, and vanilla at low speed until combined. (Some pieces of butter will remain.) Switch to dough hook attachment; gradually add remaining 1½ cups flour, beating until a dough forms and pulls away from sides of bowl.
3. Turn out dough onto a lightly floured surface, and knead until dough forms a smooth ball, about 8 times. Spray a large bowl with cooking spray. Place dough in bowl, turning to grease top. Cover and let rise in a warm, draft-free place (75°) until doubled in size, about 1 hour and 15 minutes.
4. Line 2 baking sheets with parchment paper.

5. Punch dough down. On a lightly floured surface, roll dough to ½-inch thickness. Using a doughnut cutter, cut doughnuts. Place 2 inches apart on prepared pans. Loosely cover, and let rise until puffy, 30 to 40 minutes.
6. Preheat oven to 375°. Uncover dough. Bake until lightly browned, about 10 minutes. Brush with melted butter. Drizzle with Cane Syrup Glaze, and sprinkle with pecans. Serve warm.

CANE SYRUP GLAZE
MAKES ABOUT 1½ CUPS

1   cup confectioners' sugar, sifted
½   cup cane syrup
½   cup light corn syrup
1   teaspoon vanilla extract

1. In a small bowl, whisk together all ingredients until combined.

IF YOU DON'T HAVE A DOUGHNUT CUTTER, CUT ROUNDS USING A 3¼-INCH ROUND CUTTER. USING A 1¼-INCH ROUND CUTTER, CUT OUT CENTERS OF DOUGH.

Essentials

KEEP THESE RECIPES HANDY AS YOU BAKE
YOUR WAY THROUGH THE SEASON

FALL BAKING | CHAPTER SIX

Caramel Sauce

MAKES ABOUT ¾ CUP

½   cup sugar
2   tablespoons water
1   tablespoon light corn syrup
1   tablespoon cold unsalted butter
⅛   teaspoon salt
½   cup heavy whipping cream

1. In a medium heavy saucepan, sprinkle sugar in an even layer. In a small bowl, stir together 2 tablespoons water and corn syrup until combined. Pour over sugar, stirring just until moistened. Cook over medium-high heat, without stirring, until golden brown.

Remove from heat. Add butter and salt, whisking until butter melts.
2. In a small microwave-safe bowl, place cream. Microwave until hot but not boiling, about 30 seconds. Whisk into caramel. (Mixture will foam.) Cook over low heat, stirring constantly, until smooth, about 1 minute. Remove from heat.
3. Pour into a medium bowl. Let cool for 10 minutes, stirring occasionally. Serve warm or chilled. Cover and refrigerate for up to 1 week.

Pumpkin Ice Cream

MAKES ABOUT 1 QUART

1½   cups whole milk
1   cup heavy whipping cream
⅔   cup granulated sugar
¼   cup firmly packed light brown sugar
⅛   teaspoon salt
5   large egg yolks
1   (15-ounce) can pumpkin
2   teaspoons pumpkin pie spice
1   teaspoon vanilla extract
Garnish: prepared pecan brittle

1. In a medium saucepan, combine milk, cream, sugars, and salt over medium heat, stirring occasionally.
2. Place egg yolks in a medium bowl; whisk in half of hot milk mixture. Transfer egg mixture to remaining milk mixture in

saucepan, whisking to combine. Cook over medium heat, stirring constantly, until mixture thickens and coats the back of a spoon. Remove from heat; stir in pumpkin. Strain pumpkin mixture through a fine-mesh sieve into a bowl. Add pumpkin pie spice and vanilla to pumpkin mixture, whisking to combine. Cover and refrigerate until thoroughly chilled, about 4 hours.
3. Freeze pumpkin mixture in an ice cream maker according to manufacturer's instructions. Spoon into a freezer-safe container. Cover and freeze until firm, about 3 hours. Serve with pecan brittle, if desired.

Pear-Apple Butter

MAKES ABOUT 3 CUPS

4   cups peeled, cored, and coarsely chopped pear
4   cups peeled, cored, and coarsely chopped cooking apple, such as Braeburn
1   cup firmly packed light brown sugar
¼   cup apple cider
1   teaspoon ground cinnamon
¼   teaspoon ground nutmeg
⅛   teaspoon salt
1   tablespoon fresh lemon juice
1   teaspoon peeled grated fresh ginger

1. In a large saucepan, bring pear, apple, brown sugar, cider, cinnamon, nutmeg, and salt to a boil over medium-high heat. Reduce heat to medium-low; partially cover and simmer, stirring occasionally, until very tender, about 30 minutes. Remove from heat; let cool for 10 minutes.
2. Spoon mixture into the work bowl of a food processor; process until smooth. Return mixture to saucepan. Bring to a boil, uncovered, over medium-high heat. Reduce heat to medium-low; simmer, stirring occasionally, until mixture has thickened and most of liquid has evaporated, about 7 minutes. Stir in lemon juice and ginger. Let cool to room temperature.
3. Spoon into glass jars. Store in refrigerator for up to 1 month. Stir before serving.

Homemade Pumpkin Spice

MAKES ABOUT ¼ CUP

3   tablespoons ground cinnamon
1   tablespoon ground nutmeg
1   tablespoon ground ginger
2   teaspoons ground allspice

1. In a small bowl, stir together all ingredients until combined. Store in an airtight container for up to 1 year.

Apple Cider Syrup

MAKES ABOUT 1 CUP

1   quart apple cider

1. In a small Dutch oven, bring apple cider to a boil over medium-high heat. Cook, stirring occasionally, until cider reduces to 1 cup, about 40 minutes. Pour into a bowl. Serve warm, or let stand until cooled. (Syrup thickens as it cools.) Refrigerate for up to 2 weeks